# A Cognitive-Behavioral Approach
# to the Beginning of the End of Life

✓Treatments *That Work*™

# A Cognitive-Behavioral Approach to the Beginning of the End of Life

**MINDING THE BODY**

*Facilitator Guide*

Jason M. Satterfield

OXFORD
UNIVERSITY PRESS

2008

# OXFORD

### UNIVERSITY PRESS

Oxford University Press, Inc., publishes works that further
Oxford University's objective of excellence
in research, scholarship, and education.

Oxford   New York
Auckland   Cape Town   Dar es Salaam   Hong Kong   Karachi
Kuala Lumpur   Madrid   Melbourne   Mexico City   Nairobi
New Delhi   Shanghai   Taipei   Toronto

With offices in
Argentina   Austria   Brazil   Chile   Czech Republic   France   Greece
Guatemala   Hungary   Italy   Japan   Poland   Portugal   Singapore
South Korea   Switzerland   Thailand   Turkey   Ukraine   Vietnam

Published by Oxford University Press, Inc.
198 Madison Avenue, New York, New York 10016

www.oup.com

Oxford is a registered trademark of Oxford University Press

Library of Congress Cataloging-in-Publication Data
Satterfield, Jason M.
A cognitive-behavioral approach to the beginning of the end of life :
minding the body : facilitator guide / Jason M. Satterfield.
p. ; cm. — (TreatmentsThatWork)
Includes bibliographical references.
ISBN 978-0-19-534163-8 (alk. paper)
1. Chronic diseases—Psychological aspects.   2. Terminal care—
Psychological aspects.   3. Cognitive therapy.   I. Title.   II. Series:
Treatments that work.
[DNLM:   1. Terminal Care—psychology.   2. Cognitive Therapy—
methods.   3. Stress, Psychological—therapy.   4. Terminally Ill—
psychology. WB 310 S253c 2008]
RC108.S28 2008
616'.029—dc22                                    2007043885

Printed in the United States of America

# About Treatments *ThatWork*™

Stunning developments in healthcare have taken place over the last several years, but many of our widely accepted interventions and strategies in mental health and behavioral medicine have been brought into question by research evidence as not only lacking benefit but perhaps inducing harm. Other strategies have been proven effective using the best current standards of evidence, resulting in broad-based recommendations to make these practices more available to the public. Several recent developments are behind this revolution. First, we have arrived at a much deeper understanding of pathology, both psychological and physical, which has led to the development of new, more precisely targeted interventions. Second, our research methodologies have improved substantially, such that we have reduced threats to internal and external validity, making the outcomes more directly applicable to clinical situations. Third, governments around the world and healthcare systems and policymakers have decided that the quality of care should improve, that it should be evidence based, and that it is in the public's interest to ensure that this happens (Barlow, 2004; Institute of Medicine, 2001).

Of course, the major stumbling block for clinicians everywhere is the accessibility of newly developed evidence-based psychological interventions. Workshops and books can go only so far in acquainting responsible and conscientious practitioners with the latest behavioral healthcare practices and their applicability to individual patients. This new series, Treatments *ThatWork*™, is devoted to communicating these exciting new interventions to clinicians on the frontlines of practice.

The manuals and workbooks in this series contain step-by-step detailed procedures for assessing and treating specific problems and diagnoses. But this series also goes beyond the books and manuals by providing ancillary materials that will approximate the supervisory process in assisting practitioners in the implementation of these procedures in their practice.

In our emerging healthcare system, the growing consensus is that evidence-based practice offers the most responsible course of action for the mental health professional. All behavioral healthcare clinicians deeply desire to provide the best possible care for their patients. In this series, our aim is to close the dissemination and information gap and make that possible.

This facilitator guide, and the corresponding workbook for clients, is designed to help individuals cope with chronic and/or terminal diseases. Its focus is on care rather than cure. While these patients' diseases may not be cured nor their lives prolonged, their suffering can be reduced while supporting their mental, social, and spiritual health. Quality of life deserves as much mindful attention as quantity of life.

This collaborative, skill-based program addresses the emotional, psychosocial, and spiritual needs of patients. It uses a flexible, modular format that can be adapted to best suit each client. Sessions cover stress, mood, and symptom management. Clients may work on improving social support and communication skills. This program also addresses practical concerns about medical care and explores spiritual issues. It includes goal setting and a broad assortment of cognitive-behavioral techniques. Those working with this population will find this book an indispensable guide to help patients adjust to their conditions and begin to prepare for the end of life.

David H. Barlow, Editor-in-Chief,
Treatments *ThatWork*™
Boston, Massachusetts

## References

Barlow, D. H. (2004). Psychological treatments. *American Psychologist,59*, 869–878.

Institute of Medicine (2001). *Crossing the quality chasm: A new health system for the 21st century.* Washington, DC: National Academy Press.

# Contents

**Module 4: Quality of Life**

# Acknowledgments

I would like to gratefully acknowledge the support and valuable input from numerous individuals and groups that helped make this book a reality. This program is the culmination of several years of research and clinical experience initially developed and delivered by the University of California, San Francisco (UCSF) Comprehensive Care Team. This interdisciplinary team was made possible by the generous financial support of the Robert Wood Johnson Foundation. From the prescience of its program directors—Drs. Michael Rabow and Stephen McPhee—and the synergies of the team members (Karen Schanche, Celi Adams, Ron Finley, Sue Dibble, Jason Satterfield, Jane Petersen, Cindy Perlis, and Rod Seeger) emerged the basis of what has become a thriving palliative care service at UCSF Medical Center. The UCSF Division of General Internal Medicine is to be commended for its early recognition of the importance of psychosocial factors in end-of-life care and its ongoing commitment to social and behavioral health in primary care.

A debt of gratitude is also owed to the many cognitive-behavioral therapy researchers, teachers, and clinicians who have collectively evolved an impressive toolbox of therapeutic interventions. Without their commitment, dedication, and clinical wisdom we would not have the promise of improving the quality of life in this important client population. Special gratitude goes to Drs. Marty Seligman, Aaron (Tim) Beck, Rob DeRubeis, Ricardo Muñoz, Pat Areán, Jackie Persons, and Jane Eldridge.

My greatest debt of gratitude is owed to the many patients and families who have participated in various aspects of this treatment program. The final product is very much enhanced and improved as a consequence of their insight, sensitivity, and selfless desire to help others even at a time when they were quite ill.

On a more personal note, I have learned from patients that our relationships are our most precious resource. It is only through the support from those relationships that endeavors such as this are made possible. Appreciation goes to Homer Perez, Kiersten Wells, Jeff Satterfield, and Rachel (Satterfield) Owen. A special heartfelt thank you goes to Karl Banta for his unwavering support, patience, and exuberance.

Jason M. Satterfield

# Introductory Information for Facilitators

## Background Information and Purpose of This Program

The unprecedented advances in twentieth-century biomedicine gave rise to a transformation in how medical providers and the public thought about the end of life. Death became an enemy to be conquered, or at least held at bay for as long as possible. As medical trainees were taught to cure illness instead of care for patients, quantity of life trumped quality of life. "High tech" replaced "high touch." One success of the high-tech approach is the irrefutable increase in life expectancy. Individuals in industrialized nations are living longer and they are dying mostly from chronic diseases that cause a gradual but eventually unstoppable decline toward death. This shift in the causes and trajectory of death, coupled with the rapidly increasing numbers of the elderly, has created an expanding need for both chronic-disease management and attention to the non-biomedical needs that arise as the end of life approaches.

With the birth of the modern hospice movement and the initial publication of scholarly works such as Kübler-Ross's *On Death and Dying*, the notion of caring for the whole patient at each stage of life including death began to regain legitimacy. Endings were seen as important as beginnings. As with birth, death required planning and preparation, and presented important and often difficult medical, psychosocial, emotional, and spiritual challenges. To meet the needs of the whole person, a multi-disciplinary team with flexible tools and resources was often required.

This treatment program was developed to assist medical providers in meeting the psychosocial, emotional, and spiritual needs of patients with advanced, chronic disease who are still well enough to actively participate in treatment—i.e., a population at the "beginning of the end of life." Although many excellent resources are available for caregivers, there are few equivalent programs for the dying person. Many of the tools provided in this treatment rely heavily on cognitive-behavioral therapy (CBT), although other diverse theoretical systems such as humanism, existentialism, family systems, pastoral counseling, thanatology, and chronic disease self-management have informed much of the overall framework and approach.

Facilitators should already have some expertise with cognitive-behavioral interventions. Master's level counselors, social workers, and nurse practitioners or others with mental health training may qualify. The basic philosophy of this program supports the hospice model of multidisciplinary end-of-life care but brings mental health and other psychosocial concerns to the foreground. Ideally, multidisciplinary team comanagement of clients will occur. It is recommended that all facilitators of any level have regular consultations and support depending on their level of competence and the level of difficulty the client's situation presents. Fidelity checklists have been included in an appendix for convenience. Each checklist includes an outline of the corresponding session and space for notes. Facilitators may want to use this as part of the supervision process or to rate self-adherence. Facilitators may also find it helpful to record time estimates for each session element. Forms from the book may be photocopied as needed.

## Disorder or Problem Focus

Life is a terminal condition. Although cause, timing, and circumstances may vary greatly, everyone must eventually face this normative stage of life. This program was developed to assist adult clients who have serious, progressive illnesses that will most likely result in their death. In this circumstance, these individuals have the opportunity to prepare for their death and exert some control over the rate and intensity of their decline. It is important to note that this program does not address terminally ill children.

Chronic illnesses that are the leading causes of death include heart disease, stroke, pulmonary disease, cancer, and diabetes. Related contributors include obesity, high blood pressure, high cholesterol, smoking, and excessive alcohol use (McGinnis & Foege, 1993). High comorbid levels of chronic stress, depression, and anxiety may amplify psychosocial impairment and actually hasten the biomedical progression of disease (Adler & Matthews, 1994).

This program targets a wide range of issues that commonly occur during the course of a serious illness. These issues include stress and coping, depression, anxiety, anger, social support, communication, working with medical providers, symptom management, and spirituality. It is important to remember that most clients will not become clinically depressed nor develop other new psychiatric disorders at the end of life. However, many will face adjustment challenges and may benefit from both the practical and emotional support provided by this program. As an overarching goal, this program aims to maximize the quality of life at the end of life by alleviating unnecessary suffering and facilitating the achievement of whatever the client may deem a "good death."

## Assessment and Diagnosis

Before beginning treatment, it will be essential to perform a thorough assessment and diagnostic workup. Given the range of issues that may arise, multiple assessment tools should be used to capture both possible psychopathology and more general issues in coping and adjustment. It is important to remember that every client will have a serious biomedical condition that may influence their performance on various assessments—e.g., scores for fatigue, insomnia, or weight loss may be due to a medical condition and not psychiatric impairment.

This program is intentionally designed to offer flexibility in focus, intensity, and duration based on assessment results. Data from assessments should be used to inform treatment planning, goal setting, and targets for initial self-monitoring exercises. (For group, couples, and other format variations see the chapter Program Adaptations at the end of this book.) Initial intake results should be shared with the client during the first session. Clients should participate in ongoing self-assessments and treatment modifications as the program progresses. Further discussion of assessment issues and suggested tools can be found in the next chapter (Assessment).

## Diagnostic Criteria for Adjustment Disorders

In the following outline we list the *Diagnostic and Statistical Manual of Mental Disorders* (4th ed., text revised) (DSM-IV-TR; American Psychiatric Association, 2000) criteria for adjustment disorders. Please note that clients may meet criteria for other disorders including major depression or generalized anxiety. However, most clients at the beginning of the end of life will not have a new psychiatric diagnosis. Any prior history of psychiatric impairment or substance abuse should be assessed in order to gauge possible prognosis and target interventions to prevent relapse.

### Diagostic Criteria for Adjustment Disorders

A. The development of emotional or behavioral symptoms in response to an identifiable stressor(s) occurring within 3 months of the onset of the stressor(s).

B. These symptoms or behaviors are clinically significant as evidenced by either of the following:
    1. Marked distress that is in excess of what would be expected from exposure to the stressor
    2. Significant impairment in social or occupational (academic) functioning

C. The stress-related disturbance does not meet the criteria for another specific Axis I disorder (clinical disorder) and is not merely an exacerbation of a preexisting Axis I or Axis II disorder (personality disorder or mental retardation).

D. The symptoms do not represent bereavement.

E. Once the stressor (or its consequences) has terminated, the symptoms do not persist for more than an additional 6 months.

Specify if:

A. **Acute:** if the disturbance lasts less than 6 months

B. **Chronic:** if the disturbance lasts for 6 months or longer

Adjustment disorder subtypes are selected according to the predominant symptoms:

- With depressed mood

- With anxiety

- With mixed anxiety and depressed mood

- With disturbance of conduct

- With mixed disturbance of emotions and conduct

- Unspecified

## Development and Evidence Base for This Program

This program was initially developed in 1998 as part of a larger multi-disciplinary project funded by the Robert Wood Johnson Foundation and directed by Michael Rabow, MD. This project created a Comprehensive Care Team (CCT) at the University of California, San Francisco, to deliver evidence-based health care to clients at the "beginning of the end of life" (Rabow, Dibble, Pantilat, & McPhee, 2004). CCT participants were seriously ill, adult medical patients who were actively pursuing treatment of their disease as outpatients at UCSF. Patients had advanced cancer, congestive heart failure, or chronic obstructive pulmonary disease with prognoses ranging from 1 to 5 years. Fifty patients were enrolled in the intervention condition and forty patients served as controls. Since part of the intervention included physician education and training, randomization occurred on the level of the physician clinic and not by patient.

Intervention patients were offered a large menu of options including palliative care consultations, pain management, social services, spiritual counseling, art experientials, and the Minding the Body psychosocial treatment program. The overall intent of the CCT was to demonstrate the feasibility and clinical utility of creating specialized consultations and clinical care for this patient population. The CCT did not test the stand-alone efficacy of the Minding the Body program nor that of any of the other CCT constituent elements. Results from this study showed improved outcomes in dyspnea, anxiety, sleep, and spiritual well-being but failed to improve pain, depression, or quality of life (Rabow, Dibble, et al., 2004). Primary care providers' failure to follow consultation recommendations and the relatively low enrollment and attendance to the psychosocial treatment elements may have limited gains in these areas. Informally, patients cited transportation problems, uncontrolled pain, and anxiety about group participation as primary obstacles to the Minding the Body program.

As the CCT psychologist, Dr. Satterfield developed an evidence-based, manualized, group treatment called "Minding the Body." Although participants were not required to meet DSM-IV criteria for clinical depression or anxiety, CBT interventions were used as a basis for teaching mood management and ways of coping. Given the importance of social supports in this population, sessions on communication and conflict resolution were added. Practical information for symptom management and working with medical providers were later included based on participant feedback and the success of a local caregiver training program, Home Care Companions directed by Celi Adams, RN. A final session on spirituality was developed with input from the CCT chaplain, Rev. Rod Seeger. Participant input was used to improve cultural sensitivity and acceptability throughout.

Given the breadth of skills introduced in Minding the Body, the program was framed as a sampler of introductory skills that would assist participants in selecting the most personally relevant skills for further development in more focused programs or in individual counseling. After several group iterations, the format was changed from group to individual counseling to provide more one-on-one support and best tailor the program to the needs of the individual. Individual treatment based on Minding the Body ranged from 4 to 24 sessions and sometimes included telephone and Internet counseling. Both group and individual formats were facilitated by a doctoral-level psychologist, although elements of the program have since been used by master's level social workers, counselors, psychiatric nurses, and chaplains. Further variations, adaptations, and group logistics are discussed in the chapter Program Adaptations.

A review of all of the seminal studies supporting CBT for mood disorders, stress, and other conditions is beyond the scope of this chapter. However, several key studies and treatment programs provided important foundational elements. The cognitive theory of stress and coping (Lazarus & Folkman, 1984) and the Coping Effectiveness Training (CET) program (Chesney, Chambers, Taylor, Johnson, & Folkman, 2003) were the basis for the stress management and coping skills sections. CET was effective in improving coping and mood in a distressed HIV population (Chesney et al., 2003). The depression and other mood management strategies were heavily influenced by the empirically supported work of Ricardo Muñoz and others at San Francisco General Hospital (Muñoz and Miranda, 1994; Muñoz et al., 1995). Other key influences include the cognitive work of Aaron Beck and colleagues (Beck, Rush, Shaw, & Emery, 1979) and problem-solving therapy by Nezu (1986) and Areán (2001). Empirical support or conceptual foundations for particular exercises are listed in the relevant chapters throughout this text.

Other empirical studies have shown that psychosocial interventions in similar populations are efficacious. For example, relaxation training is effective for clients with cancer, chronic obstructive pulmonary disease (COPD), or congestive heart failure (Burish & Jenking, 1992; Chang et al., 2005; Gift, Moore, & Soeken, 1992). Stress management training improves quality of life and other outcomes in breast cancer survivors or elderly clients with heart failure (Antoni et al., 2006; Luskin, Reitz, Newell, Quinn, & Haskell, 2002). More generally, CBT interventions have been effectively used for COPD, cancer pain, cancer symptom management, and associated functional limitations (Dalton, Keefe, Carlson, & Youngblood, 2004; Doorenbos et al., 2005; Kunik et al., 2001; Sherwood et al., 2005).

The core skills and ideas introduced in this program include the following:

### Meta-Cognitive

- Self-monitoring

- Goal setting

- Problem solving

- Cognitive restructuring

- Directed/balanced attention

- Savoring

### Interpersonal

- Communication skills

- Conflict resolution and negotiation

- Building intimacy

- Acceptance

- Forgiveness

- Expressing gratitude

### Behavioral

- Activity scheduling

- Graded task assignment

- Somatic quieting

- Breathing

- Progressive muscle relaxation

- Guided imagery

- Expressive writing

### End-of-Life or Disease Related

- Chronic disease self-management

- Working with a medical team

- Symptom management—pain, insomnia, fatigue, nausea

- Addressing legal issues

- Exploring spirituality

- Leaving a legacy

- Facilitating a "good death"

## CBT Models

There are a number of CBT models contained throughout this program. Participants begin by learning the interdependence of cognition, behavior, and emotion and how this triad relates to social relationships, spirituality, and physical and mental health (Sessions 1 and 2). The cognitive model of stress—stressors, appraisals, and ways of coping—is introduced in Sessions 2 and 3 along with a model of effective problem solving. Cognitive models of depression, anxiety, and anger are presented in Sessions 4–6, respectively. Basic cognitive and problem-solving skills are applied to improving relationships, working with medical professionals, and managing symptoms in later sessions.

## A Caveat about This Treatment Program

As with any type of CBT, the facilitator is expected to be an active, flexible partner who presents a transparent treatment plan and rationale. Interventions are evidence based when possible, but important concepts should be illustrated with salient clinical stories or examples that facilitate client identification and integration of the material. It is essential, however, to remember that there is no correct way of approaching the end of life. Although a common goal of reducing suffering and maximizing quality may be shared, what those outcomes might look like will vary greatly depending on culture, family background, religion, and other factors. A key tenet of this program is empowering and inspiring the client (and loved ones) to create his or her own vision of what a good death might be, then developing the structured steps to promote its achievement. For some, it may not be possible to have the kind of "good death" they desire. Personalities, social histories, or other circumstances may intervene in ways that cannot be overcome. Other clients may not be ready to face this difficult life stage and may withdraw after a few initial sessions. It is important to remember that program participants are not necessarily on "death's door" but they are probably battling the disease that will eventually kill them. A careful balance between instilling hope and facing reality will need to be found for each client.

Although the skills acquired may reduce some physical symptoms and could feasibly prolong life, it is important that clients not see this program as a pathway to a miracle cure. This manual emphasizes quality of life and makes no claims about quantity. It aims to promote the mindful consideration and response to critical end-of-life issues while teaching practical skills of stress management and emotional regulation. The Minding the Body program has often instilled hope in its participants but in a spirit of "expect the best but be prepared and able to accept the worst."

Since the overall program is conceived as a "sampler course" for various CBT skills and end-of-life issues, each session contains references for clients interested in further exploration. The final session contains a more robust list of references and resources to assist clients in planning next steps.

A "Frequently Asked Questions," or "FAQ" section appears at the end of each chapter. These sections illustrate actual questions from client-graduates with sample facilitator responses.

## The Role of Medical Care and Medications

This program is intended to be an adjunctive treatment to regular biomedical care for serious illness. It is not intended to replace the sometimes vast number of medications and medical procedures needed to slow the progression of chronic disease.

Medications are essential in the management of most serious medical illnesses and should be continued during this program. Clients may also opt to use medications to manage depression, anxiety, anger, or stress-related somatic symptoms such as insomnia. In each relevant session, the option of medications is discussed. Given the client population, special consideration should be given to drug–drug interactions and liver toxicity. Some medical providers would argue that for clients near the end of life, worries about chemical dependence should be minimal and drugs such as psychostimulants should move up higher in the treatment algorithm. As mentioned in the Assessment and Diagnosis section above, it will be important for the facilitator to know what medications the client is taking and how they might impact his or her ability to participate in treatment.

## Cultural Considerations

It is important to acknowledge that both CBT and end-of-life care as currently practiced in the United States are primarily the products of one dominant, cultural tradition. At its core, CBT can be a very deterministic and individually focused treatment that implicitly values self-control, will power, and direct confrontation with environmental challenges. Clients are expected to pick themselves up by their bootstraps and/or gracefully accept stressors that cannot be changed. The emphasis in CBT on empirical research may also have the unintended effect of directing efforts away from "softer" issues such as spirituality, love, or meaning. Fortunately, exciting advancements are under way to make CBT more culturally sensitive and effective in an increasingly diverse population (Hayes & Iwamasa, 2006; Sue & Sue, 2007). Significant others, family, and caregivers can be involved in the decision-making process and may choose to participate throughout this program. Sessions on relationships, spirituality, meaning, and transcendence are included to broaden the scope of CBT interventions and support the needs of clients who may come from a more collectivistic perspective. This program does assume a global attitude of hope and empowerment; however, the ways in which that hope is made manifest may vary greatly by client and family.

In the context of end-of-life medicine, cross-cultural conflicts typically arise in three core areas: sharing "bad" news, decision making, and attitudes toward end-of-life care (Kagawa-Singer & Blackhall, 2001; Searight & Gafford, 2005). Typically, a physician will first trigger these possible conflicts when presenting a diagnosis and making initial care decisions. These issues may also emerge at any time during this program, but particularly in the sessions covering subjective perception of prognosis, advanced directives, goal setting, spirituality, and meaning.

Although complex, culture should be embraced as a central aspect of the client's identity that will inform how the therapeutic relationship is experienced and how meaning is created out of sickness, suffering, and death. Interventions delivered with the best of intent may be perceived as impolite, disrespectful, or harmful. For example, written advanced directives may be seen as intrusive. Advocacy for a "do not resuscitate order" could be seen as a discrimination-based refusal of care. For the facilitator, it is essential to regularly revisit the assumptions made throughout the course of treatment—e.g., decision making should be autonomous, the needs of the individual are paramount, suffering should be avoided, truth-telling is always honorable, or clients should accept being a "burden." By including cultural factors in the initial assessment and explicitly acknowledging cultural experiences and perspectives as treatment progresses, the facilitator delivers a clear message that culture matters. While specific knowledge about different cultural groups can be helpful, even the most experienced facilitators cannot be knowledgeable of or "competent" in every culture they might encounter. However, an attitude of cultural humility and a habit of lifelong learning will assist the facilitator in remaining mindful of personal bias while learning important details of the client's cultural experience.

## Special Issues around the End of Life

Mental health and other health care professionals are paying more attention to psychosocial issues at the end of life (Werth & Blevins, 2006). Although more traditional forms of CBT and other therapies can inform the psychosocial care for this population, there are several special issues to consider. First, the traditional notion of therapist–client boundaries has been challenged. While traditional standards of ethical conduct still apply, boundaries may grow more flexible regarding nonsexual touch (e.g., hand-holding, comforting), strict adherence to administrative rules (e.g., missed appointments, having a session at a client's home), and personal self-disclosure. The spiritual and existential issues activated near the end of life may also present new and uncomfortable situations that require nontraditional therapeutic tools. Given the likelihood of boundary blurring and sometimes confusion, it is critical to seek professional consultations particularly when facilitators are new to this type of work.

Special ethical considerations may also emerge when working with patients approaching the end of life. Issues might include rules for confidentiality if a client becomes incapacitated or dies, issues around withdrawal or refusals of medical care, reports of elder or dependent-adult abuse, requests for narcotics, or a client's desire to hasten death as a way to end suffering. The American Psychological Association (APA) Ethics Code (2002) and the APA Ad Hoc Committee on End of Life Issues provide important guidance regarding these complex scenarios. The more traditional medical ethics guidelines for patient autonomy, beneficence, non-maleficence, and justice are described more fully by the ethics manual of the American College of Physicians and other sources (ACP, 1989; Kinlaw, 2005).

Given the nature of this difficult but rewarding work, special attention should be given to countertransference and therapist wellness. As always, therapists should use their own emotional reactions as diagnostic information about the client. However, cognitive therapy techniques should be self-applied in order to understand idiosyncratic areas of vulnerability and unresolved existential dilemmas. It is not uncommon for this work to reactivate unresolved grief, guilt, and/or memories of personal suffering experienced by the facilitator and/or her loved ones. The strategies for mood and stress management may offer important directions for coping and wellness for therapist as well as patient. A clinic team or other external support system familiar with end-of-life work can also provide a much-needed outlet and source of support.

## Outline of This Treatment Program

This program is meant to be maximally flexible regarding the sequence of sessions and the depth in which each session is covered. Depending on client needs, particular sessions may be repeated while others can be skipped entirely (e.g., a clinically depressed client may spend several weeks on the depression and stress sessions but skip the session on anger and forgiveness). Treatment format may also be switched to group, couples, family, telephone therapy, or other indicated adaptations as discussed in Program Adaptations at the end of the book.

Conceptually, the program is divided into four modules that deepen and elaborate core material longitudinally. Although sessions may be shuffled as needed, it may be easiest to shuffle modules rather than individual sessions. Module 1 (Sessions 1–3) covers stress, appraisals, and coping. Core skills include cognitive exercises, diaphragmatic breathing, and pleasant activities. Module 2 (Sessions 4–6) teaches emotional management skills for depression, anxiety, and anger. Module 3 (Sessions 7–8) focuses on social support, communication, and conflict resolution. Module 4 (Sessions 9–11) includes interventions that target quality of life such as symptom management, completing unfinished business, and spirituality. Maintenance or "booster sessions" should be considered even for clients who demonstrate substantial pre- to post-treatment gains. As with any skill-building program, it is helpful to revisit and recalibrate new behaviors.

**Table 1.1 Outline of Program**

| Modules | Sessions |
| --- | --- |
| Stress and Coping | Session 1—Medical Illness and Stress<br>Session 2—Stress, Thinking, and Appraisals<br>Session 3—Coping with Stress: Problem-Focused and Emotion-Focused Strategies |
| Mood Management | Session 4—Illness and Mood: Depression<br>Session 5—Illness and Mood: Anxiety<br>Session 6—Illness and Mood: Anger |
| Social Supports | Session 7—Social Support Network<br>Session 8—Communication and Conflict Resolution |
| Quality of Life | Session 9—Management of Medical Symptoms<br>Session 10—Quality of Life: Setting Goals and Looking Forward<br>Session 11—Resilience, Transcendence, and Spirituality |

The corresponding workbook will aid facilitators in delivering this program. Each session in the facilitator guide corresponds to a chapter in the client workbook. Clients will need to bring their workbooks to every session and are encouraged to make notes. Some workbook exercises will be started in session then completed in between visits. Other exercises will be done entirely on the client's own time. The workbook contains all key figures, psychoeducation, and instructions for various relaxation strategies. It includes basic forms for thought records, problem solving, and activity scheduling, plus a number of other structured worksheets to guide the client in self-discovery and goal setting. All forms intended for multiple use can be photocopied from the workbook or downloaded from the Treatments*ThatWork*™ Web site at www.oup.com/us/ttw.

# Assessment

Given the breadth of this program and the range of potential client needs and goals, a standard battery of assessment tools is impractical. To assist facilitators in selecting the tools to use with each client, this chapter lists major assessment categories and suggested intake instruments. It is recommended that a few "broad-spectrum" screening questions (e.g., quality of life or general coping) be used, followed by more in-depth assessment tools, depending on which issues may be most relevant. These assessments should be conducted prior to beginning the program and the results reviewed with the client during the first session. The client's medical condition should be taken into account when scoring (e.g., fatigue, insomnia, weight loss, etc. may be due to a medical condition and not psychiatric impairment). Data from assessments should be used to inform treatment planning, goal setting, and targets for initial self-monitoring exercises. The type and frequency of repeated assessments should be based on treatment goals, client interest, and feasibility.

## Biology

If possible, the client should provide a release of information that allows medical records to be shared with the program facilitator. Medical information should include primary medical diagnoses, prognosis, health status, functional impairments, chief symptoms and severity (including pain, dyspnea, nausea, fatigue), medications, and ongoing medical interventions. It is possible that key medical symptoms have gone untreated or are poorly managed (e.g., pain is regularly a 6 out of 10). If this is the case, the first intervention should be to advocate for effective symptom management. Basic needs such as nutrition, sleep, shelter, safety, cognitive function, and controlling pain are critical first steps before moving to "higher" needs on the Maslow hierarchy (Maslow, 1943).

## Psychology

### Stress and Coping

An initial baseline measure of psychosocial stress and ways of coping will assist in determining stress management goals and interventions. Most measures of stress (e.g., life events surveys or hassles scales) are lengthy and difficult to score. The Perceived Stress Scale (Cohen, Kamarck, & Mermelstein, 1983) is a short, 10-item instrument that may capture stress related to affective and physical symptoms but only partially correlates with life events. The Impact of Events Scale (IES; Zilberg et al., 1982) measures the stress encountered when a person is faced with a difficult life event, and the IES has been used with breast cancer patients (Spiegel et al., 1999). The Ways of Coping Questionnaire (Folkman & Lazarus, 1988) is the most complete and commonly used coping measure. However, its length and complex 8-factor scoring limit its utility in a busy clinical setting. The Brief COPE is perhaps a more realistic alternative coping questionnaire, given its short length and focus on highest yield questions (Carver, 1997).

### Cognition, Memory, Concentration

Delirium, dementia, and more subtle forms of cognitive impairment are not unusual in clients approaching the end of life. Although many behavioral interventions in this manual can be used with cognitively impaired clients, the program assumes a normal level of intellectual functioning. The most commonly used tool to detect serious cognitive impairment is the clinician-administered Mini-Mental Status Examination (Folstein, Robins, & Helzer, 1983). As in any treatment program, language ability and literacy should also be assessed.

## Emotion and Mood

There may be considerable overlap between the client's biomedical illness and symptoms related to a mood disorder or more general distress. With this population, many clinicians use their preferred depression and anxiety assessment tools but disregard or de-emphasize the somatic or neurovegetative symptoms (e.g., fatigue, appetite, sleep) when scoring. The 11-item version of the Profile of Mood States (POMS; Cella et al., 1987) provides a reasonable measure of general distress and has been used in terminally ill populations.

## Depression

It has been suggested that depressive cognitive symptoms (e.g., hopelessness, worthlessness, guilt) and global anhedonia show the greatest utility in evaluating the presence of depression in this population. While a client's activity levels may have dropped due to medical disease, nondepressed clients will redirect their attention and enjoyment to less physically demanding activities. Depressed clients will be unable to enjoy any activities regardless of physical ability. Commonly used depression instruments include the Zung Self-Rating Depression Scale (Zung, 1967), the Geriatric Depression Scale (Yesavage, 1982), and the Beck Depression Inventory (Beck et al., 1961). A 3-item version of the Hopelessness Scale has also shown good validity and reliability in terminally ill patients (Abbey, Rosenfeld, Pessin, & Breitbart, 2006; Beck, Weissman, Lester, & Trexler, 1974).

## Anxiety

In this population, anxiety may have many etiologies and manifestations. Uncontrolled pain, hypoxia, drug side effects, or withdrawal can cause what appears to be anxiety. Existential or more general fears about this life stage may also manifest somatically. Conditioned fears such as anticipatory nausea and vomiting in post-chemotherapy clients may also be present. Instruments such as the Beck Anxiety Inventory (Beck et al., 1988) or the State-Trait Anxiety Inventory (Spielberger et al., 1968) provide a general measure of possible somatic and cognitive manifestations of anxiety, but further questioning may be needed to determine the etiology and plan treatment accordingly.

## Anger

There are a number of instruments that assess different aspects of anger—e.g., hostility, cynicism, aggression, intensity, modes of expression, etc. The Cook-Medley Hostility Scale (derived from the Minnesota Multiphasic Personality Inventory [MMPI]) is a favorite of health psychologists and has shown predictive utility for some cardiovascular and other health events. However, it primarily taps personality characteristics or enduring beliefs related to hostility (Barefoot et al., 1989). The State-Trait Anger Scale (Spielberger et al., 1983) assesses both state anger or arousal (e.g., irritation, frustration) and trait anger (e.g., proneness to anger).

## Social Factors

The Multidimensional Scale of Perceived Social Support (MSPSS; Zimet et al., 1990) includes three subscales, each addressing a different source of support—family, friends, and significant others. The MSPSS has been linked to cardiac survival and other health outcomes (Frasure-Smith et al., 2000). The Duke–UNC Functional Social Support Questionnaire (FSSQ) is a brief measure of perceived social support developed for medical patients (Broadhead et al., 1988). Session 7 also contains collaborative exercises that will assist both client and therapist in populating a social support map and identifying the types of support available.

## Spirituality

Session 11 provides a detailed set of questions for a "psychospiritual assessment." While these questions do not provide a quantitative measure of spiritual health, they do provide guidance in exploring issues that may be critical to certain clients. For the sake of treatment planning, the intake assessment should include one to two questions regarding the importance of spirituality, such as: "Is spirituality important to you and/or your family?" or "How can we help you maintain your source of spiritual strength and meaning during this illness?" If more quantitative measures are desired, the Functional Assessment of Chronic Illness Therapy–Spiritual Well-Being Scale (FACIT-SWB), a measure of spiritual well-being that includes two subscales measuring meaning and faith, can be used (Brady et al., 1999). Both of the quality-of-life measures discussed below also contain items relevant to spirituality.

## Quality of Life

Quality of life (QOL) is a notoriously difficult construct to measure given the immense variability in how clients may define it. The McGill Quality of Life (MQOL) questionnaire is a 16-item scale with reasonable psychometrics that was designed for seriously ill clients (Cohen, Mount, Strobel, & Bui, 1995). The Missoula-VITAS QOL Index (Byock & Merriman, 1998) and the Quality of Life Enjoyment and Satisfaction Questionnaire (Q-LES-Q; Endicott, Nee, Harrison, & Blumenthal, 1993) are other commonly used QOL measures. Although not empirically validated, clients may also subjectively rate their current QOL and highest QOL in the past 2–3 years on a 1–100 scale. Clients can then list three to five factors that most contribute to or detract from their current quality of life. Session 10 discusses this construct in more depth and provides workbook exercises to assist clients in assessing and improving their QOL.

# Module 1
## Stress and Coping

# Session 1 | *Medical Illness and Stress*

*(Corresponds to session 1 of the workbook)*

## Materials Needed

- Flip chart or board
- Intake assessment results
- My Initial Program Goals form

## Outline

- Give overview of the program
- Introduce the concept of mind-body medicine
- Introduce the cycle of medical illness and stress
- Discuss stress and its symptoms
- Preview stress and coping module
- Review assessment results and set initial goals
- Conduct breathing exercise
- Assign homework

## Program Overview

Tell the client that the purpose of this program is to learn about stress, coping, and serious (perhaps terminal) medical illness. Clients will learn what causes stress, how they can manage it, and what they can do to make themselves feel better mentally, physically, and spiritually despite having a chronic and probably incurable disease. Although not all who participate in this program are "dying," most will be entering the final phase of life and will need to address serious and difficult issues.

This first session begins with a familiar and somewhat safe but important topic—stress. The intent, however, is twofold: 1) to start building a foundation of knowledge about stress and disease and 2) to begin creating a therapeutic alliance that will enable the working through of more challenging end-of-life issues in later sessions. This session will cover the basics of stress, and is followed by other sessions on managing symptoms and moods, thinking patterns, problem solving and coping, communication, social support, spirituality, and planning for the future. When clients finish the program, they will have a new set of ideas and skills to help them cope with the challenges of having a serious illness.

## Program Philosophy

The philosophy of the program includes several key elements, which should be summarized for the client. First and foremost, this is a patient-centered and relationship-centered approach to the management of the psychosocial issues surrounding serious illness. Although many patients will need to be "held" by the empathy and competence of the therapist, the patient (and possibly family) will be an active participant in the treatment, including goal setting, skill selection, symptom management, and homework assignments. Although the treatment is deeply rooted in cognitive-behavioral therapy, it also recognizes the critical importance of interpersonal relationships and the need to preserve, deepen, and resolve key social and spiritual issues when an individual nears the end of life. Consequently, there is an unabashed appreciation for the healing potential of social and spiritual relationships, including the relationship with the therapist and other medical providers.

The second central philosophical tenet of this treatment promotes the notion that despite the existential anxiety and other potential sources of suffering that emerge at the end of life, this life stage should be openly acknowledged, discussed, and even appreciated. Just as birth is seen as an important beginning worthy of much preparation and thought, dying should receive equal attention with an explicit focus on the psychosocial and other tasks of dying. Preparation for the end of life is not seen as resignation or hopelessness. In contrast, although clients may be terminally ill, the goal of this program is to assist them in achieving the highest quality of life while still living with their disease. As part of that process of improving quality, the individual will prepare for the inevitable outcome for each living being—i.e., death. Finally, in contrast to what many clients may hear from their physicians, this program does not focus on extending the quantity of life at any cost. In fact, the program emphasizes quality of life in whatever way that may be subjectively defined or achieved.

## Program Format

Explain the format of the program to the client. There are 11 weekly sessions (plus optional add-ons or booster sessions). Each session is approximately 50 minutes long. The first part of each session will review content and homework from the prior week, followed by the new topic for the day—defining stress, managing moods, dealing with symptoms, etc. The second part of the session will be spent on discussion and exercises meant to illustrate the topic for the day. Each session will correspond to a chapter in the client workbook. In between sessions, clients will be asked to think about some of the ideas discussed and to see if they can apply them to their daily lives. Since each individual client may present with different emotional, physical, and social challenges, it is important to emphasize the flexibility of the program to meet the individual's needs—i.e., some topics may be repeated or deepened while others may be condensed or skipped entirely (see results of initial assessment to assist in collaborative planning).

## Program Guidelines

Emphasize the importance of weekly attendance. Given the unpredictable nature of many chronic diseases (e.g., congestive heart failure, end-stage renal disease), patients may not be physically able to attend an appointment but still be very much in need of support. If appropriate, discuss the option of phone counseling or home visits (see Program Adaptations for more information).

Remind the client that everything discussed in session is confidential with the typical exceptions present in any form of psychotherapy. (For example, confidentiality must be broken if a patient is a danger to self or others as a consequence of a psychiatric condition, if elder or child abuse is reported, etc. Please review your state laws for further specifics.)

Stress that the rewards of the program are directly proportional to the amount of work the client is willing to invest. "Work" may include readings, self-reflection, written homework assignments, enjoyable activities, conversations with loved ones, simply taking time to relax each day, or any other way of actively practicing and engaging with the material for each session. Ask clients to bring their workbooks to every session. Encourage them to add notes, write down questions, or highlight important ideas in the workbook during the session. There will also be homework assignments each week to reinforce what was learned in session. If possible, sessions may be repeated to reinforce learning and promote greater therapeutic gains.

Clients may choose to include family and/or friends in one or more sessions or homework assignments. Discuss with the client whom he would like to involve in this program and how.

## Mind-Body Medicine

The National Institutes of Health define mind-body medicine as the "interactions among the brain, mind, body, and behavior, and the powerful ways in which emotional, mental, social, spiritual, and behavioral factors can directly affect health. It regards as fundamental an approach that respects and enhances each person's capacity for self-knowledge and self-care, and it emphasizes techniques that are grounded in this approach." (See Fig. 1.1. A copy of this diagram is included in the workbook.) Each session of this program touches upon an aspect of mind-body medicine. The focus is on "care" rather than "cure." It is assumed that even in the face of a serious and perhaps terminal illness, quality of life can often be improved, and much suffering can be reduced or elim-

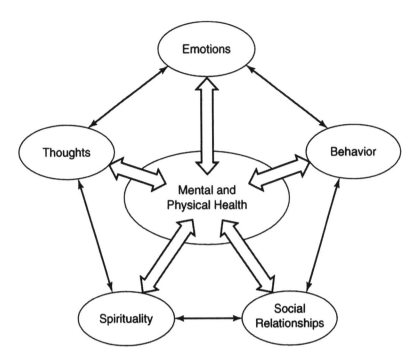

**Figure 1.1**
Mind-Body Medicine

inated. Participants will learn important mind-body skills that will help them achieve their goals and better manage their disease(s).

You may want to begin the discussion of mind-body medicine by asking clients if they are familiar with common clichés—"You are what you think," or "A healthy mind means a healthy body." For years, some medical professionals have been suggesting that the way we think and feel emotionally can affect our physical health. For the first time in history, we're starting to see empirical evidence that this is true. Provide the client with a few examples of what researchers have discovered:

■ Hostility and anger can increase the chances of having heart problems (Iribarren et al., 2000)

■ Stress and depression can suppress the immune system (Kiecolt-Glaser, McGuire, Robles, & Glaser, 2002)

■ Social support may help those with cancer to live longer (Spiegel, Bloom, Kraemer, & Gottheil, 1989)

- Stress slows wound healing and increases the risk for infection (Kiecolt-Glaser, Marucha, Marlarkey, Mercado, & Glaser, 1995)

Emphasize that thoughts can affect feelings and behavior and that this triad in turn influences social relationships and spirituality. All of these elements together can have a significant impact on physical health regardless of illness. Tell clients that throughout the course, they will work on ways to influence the way they physically feel by changing the things they do and the ways they think. They will also take a closer look at how thoughts, feelings, and behaviors influence their spirituality and social relationships.

It is important to emphasize that mind-body medicine is not about placing blame. Someone does not develop cancer (or heart disease or diabetes or other diseases) because of a bad attitude. We are biological beings and biological systems sometimes go awry or simply wear out over time. However, one's attitude in responding to illness can greatly affect one's ability to cope. Even in the case of terminal illness, mind-body medicine offers interventions that can alleviate suffering and help bring about a "good death."

## Medical Illness and Stress: A Vicious Cycle

This program begins with a focus on stress because of its almost universal occurrence and the clear mind-body links between psychological stress and medical symptoms. The management of stress can become the psychological equivalent of a "patient-controlled analgesic" imparting both symptom management and a sense of control. Explore with the client the relationship between medical illness and stress. You may want to use the following dialogue to begin:

*Serious medical illness can lead to depression, anxiety, and a lot of physical discomfort. Feeling stressed can make you more physically ill and being physically ill can make you more stressed. It's a vicious cycle if left unchecked. This program helps you manage both your stress and your illness—your mind and your body—more effectively.*

Emphasize that although this program can't cure any disease, the client can break the vicious cycle of stress and physical illness while moving ahead in coping with the important challenges of living with or dying from a serious chronic illness.

## Review of Medical Illnesses

This program is designed to help people cope with the most common chronic (and often terminal) diseases. According to the Centers for Disease Control and Prevention (CDC), the most common causes of death in the United States are heart disease, cancer, stroke, chronic obstructive pulmonary disease (COPD), accidents, and diabetes. Although these diseases and others have important differences, they share many common physical symptoms and side effects of treatment and require similar coping skills. Basic information on the top five chronic illnesses is included here for your reference. It is important for you to know the essentials of your client's disease; you may want to consult other resources as needed.

### Cancer

Cancer is actually a large group of different but related diseases characterized by the uncontrolled growth and spread of abnormal cells (i.e., tumors). The abnormal cells starve and crowd out the normal cells needed to be healthy. Common cancers are lung cancer, breast cancer, and colon cancer. Cancer may be caused by behaviors (e.g., smoking, diet, sun exposure), environmental exposures (e.g., pollution, asbestos), genetics, and/or random occurrence as normal cell division goes awry.

### Lung Disease and Chronic Obstructive Pulmonary Disease

This is a group of disorders that involves damage to the lungs and makes breathing difficult. It includes diseases such as emphysema. Many patients mistakenly call their COPD "asthma" or "bronchitis." The most common cause is smoking.

## Heart Disease

This is a collection of different diseases that affect the heart muscle and/or the blood vessels that supply the heart. Coronary artery disease (CAD) is the most common type. In CAD, blood vessels become hard and narrow allowing less blood to nourish the heart. CAD often results in angina (chest pains) and/or a myocardial infarction (i.e., heart attack). Congestive heart failure (CHF) refers to a condition in which the heart isn't able to pump enough blood to all areas of the body. This may be caused by narrowed arteries, damage to the heart muscle from a heart attack, damaged or infected heart valves or heart muscle, etc. CHF causes a variety of uncomfortable symptoms including shortness of breath and fluid retention and swelling in the legs, ankles, and feet. Fluid may also back up into the lungs, further impairing the ability to breathe, especially when lying down. Heart disease is caused by many factors including poor diet, lack of exercise, smoking, obesity, high blood pressure, high cholesterol, and genetic risk factors.

## Stroke

A stroke occurs when a blood vessel supplying the brain becomes blocked or bursts, thereby interrupting essential blood flow to a particular brain area. When this happens, brain cells are killed and serious brain damage can occur. Impairments depend on the area of brain damage but commonly include speech, memory, and movement. Risk factors include high blood pressure, high cholesterol, smoking, excessive alcohol use, and family history.

## Diabetes

Diabetes is a disease in which the body doesn't properly use or produce enough insulin. Insulin is needed to convert sugar and starches into the energy the body needs for everyday activities and to maintain a balanced level of glucose in the blood. Over time, high glucose levels can fatally damage eyes, kidneys, nerves, and the heart. Diabetes is caused by poor diet, lack of exercise, obesity, family history, and other factors.

## Common Symptoms and Stress

With the exception of some cancers, all of these diseases are incurable and potentially fatal. This program teaches ways to cope with physical and emotional symptoms, treatment side effects, and the many adjustments required as the end of life approaches. Common physical symptoms for some or all of these diseases include the following:

- Chronic pain

- Shortness of breath

- Difficulty sleeping

- Fatigue or weakness

- Loss of appetite/loss of weight

- Impaired mobility or decreased coordination

- Medication or treatment side effects (nausea, drowsiness, constipation, etc.)

Although these illnesses are very different from each other, they all cause stress and they can all be made worse by stress. Discuss the relationship between physical symptoms and stress levels. Clients should begin a personalized list of the symptoms they experience and the associated stress. The goal of this initial exercise is to begin the process of providing "hooks" and "anchors." A "hook" is a personalized way to grab and hold a patient's attention. Asking the patient to reflect on his personal experience and then showing the relevance of this program to address that experience can provide an important "hook" to promote engagement and sustain interest. An "anchor" is the patient's existing knowledge or framework on which to "hold down" additional, elaborated information or new concepts. Questions that assess the depth and accuracy of the patient's knowledge about his disease and treatment provide important data on available "anchors." Start first with disease specifics, then move to stress in the next section. Space is provided in the workbook to record the answers to the following questions.

- *What is your primary medical diagnosis?*

- *What symptoms (or side effects of treatment) are you experiencing?*

- *Do you think these symptoms or side effects can be improved? How much?*

- *How is this disease being treated?*

- *What does managing your disease require you or your loved ones to do?*

## What Is Stress?

Begin the discussion of stress by emphasizing that everyone is stressed at some point—especially if they are physically ill. Illness is not the only source of stress—work, money, children, relationship issues, or even positive events (e.g., marriage, birth of a child, move to a new city) can all contribute to stress. Events that cause stress are called "stressors." Stressors can be acute (one time) or chronic, stand alone or "chained" events, internal or external, real or imagined, in the past or anticipated in the future. We can think of stress as the tension or pressures that are a natural part of living. However, sometimes this tension can be a heavy burden to bear, particularly when mental or physical energy is at a low point. A person feels "stressed out" if the demands placed on him exceed his ability to cope.

## Categories of Stress Symptoms

Explain that stress can make its appearance through physical, behavioral, emotional, cognitive, and social symptoms. Figure 1.2 graphically demonstrates the link between a stressor and various examples of stress symptoms.

Review the following stress symptom categories with clients and ask them to reflect on their own personal experiences. Specific examples recalled from the initial intake should be used when possible.

*Physical:* shortness of breath, pounding heart, stiff or tense muscles, headaches, upset stomach, clenching jaw or fists, dizziness, trembling, diarrhea, grinding teeth, sweating, feeling faint, loss of interest in sex, tiredness, restlessness

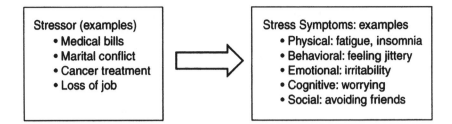

**Figure 1.2**
Stress Pathway

*Behavioral:* overeating, loss of appetite, trouble sleeping, accident proneness, using more alcohol, avoiding tasks, sleep problems, trouble completing work assignments, fidgeting, tremors, crying, smoking more

*Emotional:* irritability, anger, worry, trouble concentrating, negative attitudes, loneliness, feeling down or depressed, feeling tense, grouchiness, inability to relax

*Cognitive:* anxious or racing or slowed thoughts, fearful anticipation, poor concentration, difficulty with memory

*Social:* avoiding others, isolating, not wanting to be alone, venting, getting easily irritated with others

## Assessing Stress

A first step in effective stress management is quickly and accurately assessing personal stress levels regardless of how they manifest. Refer the client to Figure 1.2 (a copy is found in the workbook). This figure will be further elaborated as this module on stress and coping progresses. Have the client consider the following reflection questions (space is provided in the workbook to record answers).

*What are some of your primary causes of stress (i.e., stressors)?*

*How does stress affect you (physical, behavioral, emotional, cognitive, social symptoms)?*

*How can friends, family, or others tell when you are stressed?*

*What's the most stressful thing about your physical illness?*

*What makes your stress symptoms better or worse?*

Encourage clients to notice how stress symptoms may wax and wane over the next week.

## Stress and Coping Preview

Coping with stress is the quintessential example of a mind-body intervention with great potential to alleviate suffering and improve quality of life. The next two sessions will focus on more specific elements of stress and coping. For now, clients should develop an appreciation for the causes and manifestations of stress in their lives. The stress process that includes stressors, appraisals, stress symptoms, and coping will be fully mapped out in Sessions 2 and 3. A clear understanding of this process allows us to see and understand the large menu of coping opportunities available at any given time. Session 2 will cover appraisals and cognitive interventions to address inaccurate appraisals. Types of coping will be expanded upon in Session 3. Clients may begin talking about ways of coping during this session. Reinforce their foresight but encourage them to focus on the "peaks and valleys" of stress symptoms over the next week. Clients need to have a solid appreciation for the ways in which "mind" influences "body" before moving on to coping.

## Review of Assessment Results and Initial Goal Setting

In light of the recent discussion of the client's knowledge about his illness and the specifics of how he experiences stress, review the results of the assessments given prior to the first session. Although the quantity and quality of data gathered might vary, you should have some sense of the client's level of stress, depression, anxiety, anger, social supports, and quality of life. Remind the client that each of these phenomena fall within the realm of mind-body medicine and each can be changed even if the biomedical illness remains the same. With the assessment data in mind, point out what appear to be the most pressing areas for improvement (e.g., depression scores were high, social supports were low, etc.). Ask the client if he agrees with the assessment results or would like to add any new data (or reorder priorities to fit his values and interests).

Based on what the client shared in the initial assessment and what he has identified as primary stressors and stress symptoms, have the client list some initial goals using the My Initial Program Goals Form in the workbook. Areas for goal setting include medical problems, psychological issues, social and spiritual issues, and quality of life. Remember that goals should be concrete, specific, and realistic. Examples of initial goals include the following: get 6–7 quality hours of sleep per night, decrease average daily pain rating to a 4 out of 10, talk with estranged son, etc. These goals will most likely evolve over time but should give you some sense of where the client is starting and what initial goals he might have. If time permits, this exercise can be completed during Session 1. However, if time is short, this can be added to the homework exercises to be discussed at the beginning of Session 2.

## Breathing Exercise

Various methods of somatic quieting (i.e., relaxation) are an important skill set that provides clients with some immediate relief and should be practiced often. Explain that somatic quieting is an almost universally helpful way to cope with stress by relaxing the mind and body. When relaxed, it's impossible to feel tense and stressed. Diaphragmatic or belly breathing is one of the easiest ways to learn how to relax. The diaphragm is a dome-shaped muscle under the ribcage that helps fill the lungs with air when breathing deeply. The goal of this type of breathing is to regularly use the diaphragm to maximally inflate the lungs.

To conduct the breathing exercise, give the client the following instructions:

*Get into a comfortable position with the back as straight as possible (e.g., sitting up straight in a hard backed chair with feet flat on the floor). Put one hand on your stomach and the other on your chest. Inhale slowly and*

*watch which hand moves. Shallow breaths move the hand on the chest;
diaphragmatic breaths move the hand on the stomach.*

*Now, slowly inhale through your nose. As you breathe in, count slowly to 3
and feel your stomach expand with your hand. Hold the breath for 1 second. Then slowly breathe out while also counting to 3. When you inhale,
think of the word "inhale." When you exhale, think of the word "relax."*

*Inhale 1 . . . 2 . . . 3 . . . Hold 1 . . . Relax 1 . . . 2 . . . 3 . . .*

*Continue breathing in this pattern for a few minutes. Feel yourself becom-
ing more relaxed with every exhalation. Notice any changes in how your
body or mind feels. You may repeat this exercise multiple times per day.*

## Homework

✎ Have client review Session 1 of the workbook and answer the questions
in the spaces provided.

✎ Have client finish or complete the My Initial Program Goals form.

✎ Have client practice the breathing exercise on a daily basis.

## FAQs from Clients

1. Is this program only for people who are dying of some disease?

   *A: No. This program is for anyone with a serious, chronic illness. Is-
   sues of death and dying will be addressed in several chapters, but it is
   often useful for anyone of any health status to think about these issues.*

2. I'm already sick and disabled. How can you expect me to do
   more? Why can't you just take care of me?

   *A: Support and empathy, or providing care, are key parts of this pro-
   gram. However, the program session is only 1 hour per week. If you
   learn self-care skills or ways to elicit care from others, you will have
   more substantial and more sustaining care in the future. You won't be
   asked to do anything you are unable to do, but we won't know what
   you are capable of doing until you give it a try.*

3. What if this program is too hard? What if I miss sessions? Forget homework? What if I flunk out?

   *A: This program is not about getting an "A." It is not about being a good student or patient or performing in any particular way. It is an opportunity to learn important new disease management skills in a private and supportive environment. Although attendance and homework are important, no one is perfect. Do as much as you are able. If the program seems too tough, just let me know. It is designed to be flexible because people may move at different speeds and have different abilities.*

4. Should I be in a support group too? Is individual or group therapy better for me?

   *A: There are many good support groups that could be an important adjunct to this program. Support groups offer the opportunity to learn from and teach others—and maybe make some new social supports along the way. If you are able to fully participate in this program while also attending a support group, we can give you referrals. If that seems like too much, don't worry. You will still get a lot out of this individual program.*

5. Will you talk to my medical doctor(s)? Can you help me with med issues, prescriptions, referrals, etc?

   *A: Yes, I would like to talk to your medical doctors so we can coordinate your care. It is probably best to see me as a specialist in coping rather than as a primary care coordinator. I may be in a position to effectively advocate for you when issues around appointments, medications, etc. might arise. I am happy to pass along key information or make connections whenever possible. In the end, though, decisions regarding your biomedical care will still be in the hands of your physicians.*

# Session 2 | *Stress, Thinking, and Appraisals*

*(Corresponds to session 2 of the workbook)*

## Materials Needed

- Flip chart or board
- Appraisal Worksheet

## Outline

- Set the agenda
- Review homework
- Review previous session
- Introduce the cognitive component of stress management
- Present helpful (versus hurtful) ways of thinking
- Conduct helpful thoughts exercise
- Discuss common habits of mind
- Help client start to capture cognitions
- Link thinking with stress appraisals
- Conduct appraisal exercise
- Assign homework

## Setting the Agenda

Share the agenda referred to in the session outline. Collaborate with the client to set the agenda for any other relevant topics.

## Homework Review

Review the homework from the last session (i.e., stress symptom assessment, goal setting, and relaxation breathing). Homework review should always be an agenda item since the review reinforces homework completion and may highlight areas that need further clarification or practice. Identify any obstacles to completing homework and problem solve accordingly. Remind participants that homework is key to getting the most out of the program. If homework was not completed, it is important to assess why before intervening. For example, the assignment may not have been clear, the rationale may have been misunderstood, the patient may have had a flare-up of physical symptoms, etc. Some homework non-adherence is expected and should be normalized. It is important to take a collaborative, problem-solving stance to understand how to get the homework done.

Remind clients to always read the corresponding workbook chapter between sessions and complete the homework forms. Personalization of the workbook and other learning materials is encouraged. Clients may want to keep a running list of questions, requests, or comments (space is provided at the end of each workbook chapter).

## Review of Previous Session

Reiterate that the purpose of this course is to improve the quality of life for people with serious medical illnesses. A mind-body medicine approach will be used to accomplish this goal, starting with the area of stress and stress management. By the end of the program, clients will have a variety of stress management skills and other exportable tools to help themselves and their loved ones.

Briefly review the cycle of medical illness and stress. Emphasize that feeling stressed can affect the way we feel, how we think, and what we do. Review Figure 1.2 from the last session and the client's answers to the stress reflection questions. Include a discussion of the goals generated by the patient. Clarify the client's goals to make them more specific, concrete, and realistic if necessary.

## Cognitive Component of Stress Management

One major contributor to how we feel and how we cope is how we think. In fact, our feelings, thoughts, and behaviors (coping behaviors and otherwise) are intimately related (see Fig. 2.1; a copy is included in the workbook). By examining each corner of this "feeling–thoughts–behavior triangle," the client will develop a better understand of how she got where she is and what she should do to go about changing her situation.

Emphasize that the most important thing to remember about thoughts and feelings is that *they are not facts*. A thought is just an opinion—one's best guess at explaining or understanding what's going on. Opinions should always be open to reevaluation and change. A feeling (or emotion) is just a chemical signal that tells us we need to pay attention to something and possibly intervene. It grabs our attention but it doesn't prove that anything is right or wrong. (Using emotions as proof is classically called "emotional reasoning"). The feeling could easily be a false alarm based on misinformation.

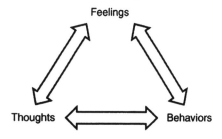

**Figure 2.1**
Feelings-Thoughts-Behavior Triangle

| $\underline{A}$ctivating Event → → → → $\underline{C}$onsequences (behaviors, emotions) |
| --- |

**Figure 2.2**
Common Perception

| $\underline{A}$ctivating Event → $\underline{B}$eliefs (thoughts) → $\underline{C}$onsequences |
| --- |

**Figure 2.3**
The A-B-Cs of Cognitive Therapy

This program seeks to teach clients the self-reflective habit of carefully considering thoughts and feelings—particularly when the stakes are substantial. To achieve this goal, clients should become very familiar with the "A-B-Cs" of cognitive therapy—i.e., how Activating ($A$) events trigger Beliefs ($B$) that contribute to emotional and behavioral Consequences ($C$). You may wish to draw these A-B-Cs on the board (see Figs. 2.2 and 2.3) and introduce the concept as follows:

> Most of us are familiar with phrases like "That doctor made me angry," or "This disease depresses me." Using our A-B-C language, these phrases claim that A, an activating event, causes C, the emotional or behavioral consequences. Although this isn't necessarily incorrect, it misses an important middle step, the step that helps us understand why people have different responses to identical situations. That middle step is B, or the beliefs and thoughts we have about the activating event. As we will learn, there is no right or wrong ways to think about an event. However, some ways of thinking are more helpful or hurtful than others.

## Helpful versus Hurtful Thinking

Describe the following elements or types of thinking to the client. The goal is to see how beliefs ($B$) can be examined and possibly changed to be more helpful (partially adapted from Muñoz et al., 1995).

## Helpful Thinking Is Balanced

Clients might see everything as the same shade of gray. They may only notice the losses, the disappointments, or the "failures." Many irreversible changes in physical function or appearance occur over the course of an illness, so it becomes difficult to see anything but losses. Remind the client that it is *very* rare for anything to be absolutely good or absolutely bad. There are always two sides to every coin. If a situation seems bad, it helps to look at the other side of the same situation or take a broader view of life. For example, rather than just thinking of things we've lost, we can also think of things we've gained. Although the client may no longer be able to visit family, rather than focus exclusively on new limits to mobility and travel, the client can appreciate that family members now come to visit her. A helpful habit to develop is always asking oneself, "What's the other side of the coin?"

Emphasize that many little positive events can add up to a significant sense of well-being. However, stress that balanced thinking is not about wearing rose-colored glasses. It is seeing both the good and the bad, feeling encouragement and discouragement. Balanced thinking is not intended to downplay the seriousness of the clients' illnesses. Their symptoms are real. Their pain may be substantial. Their fears of dying can be overwhelming. However, it is not uncommon for clients to find meaning or even inspiration in the most dire of circumstances. They change what they can, accept what they cannot, and seek to eventually find the silver lining of their illness experience. Clients may need to grieve, rage, complain, or despair. However, the goal is to eventually assist them in developing a more balanced and helpful attitude toward themselves, their illness, and their prognoses.

## Helpful Thinking Is Flexible

Things can seem unchangeable and hopeless. We may think in terms like "always" or "never." In reality, few things always stay the same, particularly if we create conditions in which change can occur. The ability to change and adapt is essential to survival and quality of life. Stress to the client the importance of keeping an open mind to information that might change her point of view. Not everything is changeable, but life is full of unexpected surprises.

Most clients will have an incurable chronic disease that may take their life at some point in the future. Their diagnoses and prognoses may seem unchangeable, so clients are tempted to simply stop trying to help themselves. Remind clients that, although their disease cannot be eradicated, there is much they can do to manage the symptoms and the side effects of treatment (e.g., pain, insomnia, diarrhea, dry mouth, fatigue). Although it may seem like they have exhausted all of the usual options, a fresh opinion or a more flexible perspective can often show the way to new ideas and interventions. This program is an example of a new opportunity for change. Hospice may also be a new conduit for hope. New medications and other treatments are regularly being discovered (e.g., HIV used to be a "death sentence," but that prognosis has dramatically changed; also, many cancers are now thought of as manageable chronic diseases).

Even if clients have maximized their symptom and side-effect management, it still behooves them to be flexible in how they think about the approach of death. We often think of death as a "bad outcome" that should always be avoided if possible. However, in the case of a chronic disease, clients have the opportunity to use their approaching death as motivation to accomplish important tasks—e.g., resolving relationships, forgiving themselves and others, expressing love, imparting wisdom, exploring spirituality, settling financial issues, etc.

## Helpful Thinking Is Nonjudgmental

In depressed thinking one often places blame on oneself or criticizes one's own character. Rather than seeing the mistake as just a mistake, this kind of thinking makes a global criticism of who one is as a person rather than what one did. Insulting oneself or others is nearly always hurtful. Encourage the client to try talking about the behavior rather than one's character. Remind the client that no one is perfect. We all have bad days and make mistakes. All we can do is take responsibility, make things right (if possible), learn, and move onward.

The issue of judgment may arise in the context of blame for a physical illness (e.g., a client with COPD or lung cancer who smoked for decades). Nonjudgmental thinking does not absolve an individual of responsibility for choices made. However, it does encourage a more compassionate and balanced look at other factors that influenced those choices (e.g., everyone in the family smoked), helps disentangle self-worth from behavior (e.g., smoking does not make one a bad person), and helps us recognize that we are all inherently flawed beings who sometimes make bad choices with bad consequences. Session 6 will explore acceptance and forgiveness in much greater depth.

## Helpful Thoughts Exercise

For this exercise, use the thoughts listed in the first column of Table 2.1. Refer the client to the copy of the table in the workbook or put the examples on a flip chart. Have the client identify what is wrong with these thoughts by circling the category or type in the second column that best describes each thought. After the client has decided on the category or type of thinking, work together to write new, more helpful thoughts to replace the original hurtful thoughts (a few examples are provided). Discuss how this relates to the A-B-Cs of cognitive therapy—i.e., although we don't know the activating events, by changing the beliefs we can change the consequences.

## Habits of Mind

In addition to unbalanced, inflexible, and judgmental thought patterns there are a number of thinking habits that we often automatically use. These "habits of mind" can all be helpful or hurtful depending on the situation. Review Table 2.2 and ask clients which of these habits sound familiar. Which sound most helpful? Most hurtful? Emphasize that everyone has habits of mind. People are not computers; we are blessed with emotions, impulses, passions, pains, and all of the joys that make life worth living. The consequence is that sometimes we need to step outside of ourselves and rethink our thinking habits (i.e., change the B in our A-B-Cs).

## Table 2.1 Helpful Thoughts Exercise

| Hurtful Thinking | Type? | New Helpful Thought |
|---|---|---|
| "I'm stupid for believing I'd get better." | Unbalanced<br>Inflexible<br>(Judgmental) | Symptoms come and go for nearly every disease. It is reasonable to hope. |
| "This pain will never relent." | Unbalanced<br>(Inflexible)<br>Judgmental | My pain is bad right now but it was better yesterday. Maybe it will change tomorrow. |
| "When it rains, it pours." | (Unbalanced)<br>Inflexible<br>Judgmental | When bad things happen, I notice other bad things too but that doesn't mean nothing good is happening. |
| "I'm too ugly to be seen in public." | Unbalanced<br>Inflexible<br>Judgmental | |
| "He'll never understand me." | Unbalanced<br>Inflexible<br>Judgmental | |
| "I'll always be disappointed." | Unbalanced<br>Inflexible<br>Judgmental | |
| "My life is falling apart." | Unbalanced<br>Inflexible<br>Judgmental | |
| "I must deserve my illness." | Unbalanced<br>Inflexible<br>Judgmental | |

## Table 2.2 Common Habits of Mind

| Magnification | Blowing things up, making them bigger than life, making mountains out of molehills |
|---|---|
| Minimization | Discounting, making molehills out of mountains |
| Personalization | Assigning personal meaning or significance to nonpersonal events, taking personal offense when none was intended |
| Mind reading | Making assumptions about what another person is thinking |
| Fortune telling | Making a prediction about what might happen in the near or distant future |
| Filtering | Selectively attending to certain details, either focusing on all negative or all positive details |
| All-or-none thinking | Seeing no shades of gray, everything seems all good or all bad, no continuum |
| Catastrophizing | Similar to magnification, imagining things are much worse than they are, assuming the worst-case scenario will come true |
| Overgeneralization | Coming to a broad conclusion based on only one or a few incidences |
| Emotional reasoning | Assuming that having a strong feeling makes something true |

Adapted from Burns (1981).

## Capturing Cognitions

In order to further develop the skills of self-reflection and cognitive re-structuring, it is important for clients to learn basic self-monitoring of cognitions and habits of mind. Define and discuss what is meant by a thought or cognition and ask the client to give a few examples of recent thoughts (e.g., thoughts while driving to the session, thoughts while doing the last homework assignment, thoughts already shared in the session). This discussion is meant to elicit a more complete understanding of the range of what can be included under the category of "cognition." Cognitions may be automatic thoughts but they might also be core beliefs, memories, images, predictions about the future, etc. regarding oneself, one's illness, one's relationships, or the world in general.

Since clients will later work on stress appraisals (a very specific type of cognition), elicit initial thoughts and responses for some or all of the following:

▩ *When you hear the name of your disease, what thought pops to mind?*

▩ *What are some thoughts you have about your treatment? About medications?*

▩ *What thoughts do you have about the way your family and friends have responded to your illness?*

▩ *What does this say about you? Your friends? Your family?*

▩ *What thoughts do you have about your ability to cope and the help you have available?*

## Linking Thinking with Stress Appraisals

Recall Figure 1.2 from Session 1, which clearly mapped the pathway between stressors and stress symptoms. Figure 2.4 builds on this model by adding appraisals (i.e., the middle step, or *B* in an A-B-C model) and coping.

Appraisals should be considered cognitions or the best guesses that clients make regarding a stressor and their coping resources. As cognitions, appraisals are subject to all of the habits of mind already discussed. A first step in stress management is tuning into the appraisals that have been made and considering whether or not these appraisals are helpful

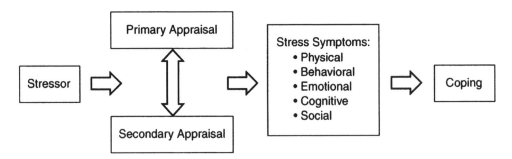

**Figure 2.4**

Stress and Coping Pathway

or hurtful. We are interested in two types of stress appraisals. *Primary appraisals* are thoughts about the stressor (e.g., does the stressor matter, is it important, how serious is it, how will it affect my life or my family, etc.). *Secondary appraisals* are best guesses about coping ability and resources (e.g., have I dealt with this before, can I handle it, do I have the skills I need to resolve this issue, are other people able to help, do I or we have the necessary time, money, and energy to fix this, etc.). Questioning appraisals is not about denial or minimizing the real problems that occur in life. However, appraisals commonly become unbalanced, inflexible, or just generally unhelpful, especially if a person is already suffering or depressed.

## Primary Appraisals (of Stressors)

Common thinking traps for primary appraisals (of stressors) include the following:

1. *Overestimating the likelihood that a bad event (stressor) will occur.* In this situation, the stressor is anticipated but hasn't actually happened (e.g., "my pain will get much worse, I will have to sit in an oxygen tent, my kids will never forgive me"). Although some worry may help us prepare for future bad events, there comes a point when worrying is just adding on more unnecessary suffering. The skills to avoid this trap include making more accurate estimations of what events will occur and deciding whether worry will help us prepare for the future.

2. *Overestimating the "badness" or negative consequences of a stressor.* In this situation, clients have catastrophized the actual or possible outcomes of a stressor. They assume that the potential consequences are much worse than they really are. They may be focusing on an unlikely worst-case scenario or they may be "awfulizing" the consequences of an anticipated stressor—e.g., "If I miss a doctor's appointment I will be dismissed from his practice and never get good medical care again."

3. *Overestimating the duration or permanence of stressor.* Chronic stressors generally cause more stress than acute stressors. Accuracy and

flexibility are key skills for avoiding the erroneous belief that things will never change (e.g., "It seemed like the nausea would never go away but the new meds and the diet change took care of it.")

4. *Considering worst-case scenarios with multiple bad outcomes.* This trap is inviting when a stressor is novel, unclear, or ambiguous. For example, when a patient first receives a diagnosis of congestive heart failure, she may picture agonizing chest pain, the feeling of drowning, chronically swollen limbs, forced early retirement, a diet of bland food, etc. Learning more about the stressor helps us have more realistic expectations about what is likely to happen and when.

Important questions to ask oneself to improve primary appraisals include the following:

- How likely is this stressor to occur?

- Is it helpful to worry about this right now?

- Have I been wrong before? Have I worried too much before?

- What are the likely outcomes if it does occur?

- How long will it last?

- How accurate have I been in the past?

- What are the best-case and worst-case scenarios?

- Can I live with the worst-case scenario?

- Could I learn more about the stressor or find someone who can answer my questions?

## Secondary Appraisals (about Coping)

Common thinking traps for secondary appraisals (about coping) include

1. Overestimating what it will take to cope with a stressor

2. Underestimating personal ability to cope with a stressor

3. Underestimating or forgetting important coping resources such as time, money, energy, knowledge, etc.

4. Underestimating or underutilizing friends, family, and others who might be willing and able to help

Important questions to ask oneself to improve secondary appraisals include the following:

- What resources are realistically needed to cope with this stressor?

- What are high and low estimates on how much of these resources will be required?

- What resources do I have at my easy disposal?

- What new resources could I possibly acquire?

- Have I coped with similar stressors in the past? How?

- Have I underestimated my ability to cope in the past?

- Who is in my social support network and what help can they provide?

- Are there new people or services I can recruit to assist with coping (e.g., social services, church help, hospice, neighbors)?

## Appraisal Exercise

If time permits, go back to the appraisals elicited under the Capturing Cognitions exercise. Have the client practice restructuring (i.e., rewriting) the appraisal into a more helpful format. Explain the Appraisal Worksheet to be used for homework (see copy of the form in the workbook). The homework is meant to give the client more practice in capturing cognitions (specifically appraisals), evaluating cognitions (i.e., are they helpful or hurtful, are they habits of mind), and restructuring cognitions. Tell clients to anticipate some difficulty, especially with the final step. An example to review is included here and in the workbook.

## Appraisal Worksheet Example

Initial situation: *Maria becomes short of breath when she walks to the mailbox. She thinks, "Oh no! I'm going downhill fast. Now I can't even walk to the mailbox. My lung disease is out of control. This is terrible!"*

Step 1: Identify the stressor

*The stressor is her perceived physical decline due to lung disease and the associated dire vision of her future.*

Step 2: Capture appraisals

Primary appraisal: *My lung disease is raging out of control. I will be housebound and helpless in a few months.*

Secondary appraisal: *There's nothing I can do cope with this. There is no cure. There is no hope.*

Step 3: Evaluate appraisals.

*Maria asks herself the list of questions for both primary and secondary appraisals (see worksheet). She assesses the accuracy of her thoughts and finds that she is catastrophizing or magnifying how bad her symptoms are or how bad they will get. She also searches for any untapped resources that she could use to help her cope.*

Step 4: Rewrite appraisals.

Primary appraisal: *Yes, my lung disease is incurable and probably progressive. But I've had peaks and valleys in the past. I have good days and bad days. Just last week I was able to play ball with my grandson without too much difficulty. I have some control over my symptoms.*

Secondary appraisal: *My oxygen really helps but I haven't been using it that often in public because it sort of embarrasses me. I can use my oxygen more regularly and I can ask my doctor to review my meds again . . . Even if I do lose more physical function, I can ask my family for more help and enjoy their support indoors. I'm blessed to have family who love me.*

## Homework

✎ Have client review the Helpful Thoughts exercise.

✎ Have client review her answers to the Capturing Cognitions exercise.

✎ Have client complete the Appraisal Worksheet.

✎ Client may choose to continue doing breathing exercises on a daily basis.

## FAQs from Clients

1. Anyone with my health problems would feel the way I feel. Are you saying this is all in my head?

   *A: Nearly everyone with a serious illness experiences stress—sometimes severe stress. But having stress does not mean it is all in your head. It simply means that your body affects your mind and vice versa. Your medical illness is very much real—it resides in your heart, lungs, blood vessels, etc. However, all of our bodily systems are connected. A heart attack will affect my mood. Having trouble breathing might make me anxious. Having a big fight with my spouse might make my back pain worse. Since you are already receiving treatment for the bodily parts of your disease, why not add treatments for your mind?*

2. Isn't this just the power of positive thinking? Isn't that a rather dated and shallow approach to a very serious problem?

   *A: Having a positive attitude is important but that's not really what this program is about. The cognitive exercises aren't about rose-colored glasses. They simply encourage you to be balanced and fair to yourself and others. We rarely have all the facts in a given situation so we are forced to make guesses. This program just asks you to look at the guesses you tend to make. Are those guesses helping you or hurting you? In later sessions, you will find that we ask you to look at some very serious and possibly painful issues. We don't encourage denial, but we do encourage being constructive and compassionate.*

3. How can I change my thoughts or my appraisals when I feel so anxious or depressed? I know I'm thinking in hurtful ways, but I just can't stop.

    *A: You're right. Changing any habit is very hard to do, especially when you are feeling physically or emotionally down. But like any new skill, things become easier with practice and good coaching. Notice where you tend to get stuck. Bring that observation to the next session and work on it with your facilitator. Remember to be balanced when evaluating your ability to do the cognitive exercises. You will have some successes, but you will almost certainly get stuck too. Practice with changing the easier (i.e., less emotionally charged) thoughts first, then moving to the more difficult levels. Practice makes perfect.*

## Session 3    *Coping with Stress: Problem-Focused and Emotion-Focused Strategies*

*(Corresponds to session 3 of the workbook)*

## Materials Needed

- Flip chart or board
- Get the Right Attitude Worksheet
- Problem Definition Worksheet
- Set Goals and Identify Obstacles Worksheet
- List Your Options Worksheet
- Pick an Option Worksheet
- Implementation and Evaluation Worksheet
- A-B-C-D Form

## Outline

- Set agenda
- Review homework
- Use appraisals to guide coping
- Discuss problem-focused coping
- Discuss emotion-focused coping
- Conduct affirmation exercise
- Introduce A-B-C-D exercise
- Assign homework

## Setting the Agenda

Set the agenda by referring to the session outline. Ask the client if any other topics should be added. If the agenda becomes too long, collaboratively prioritize the items. If time permits, it may be helpful to divide today's material into two sessions. Part 1 would cover problem-focused coping with more practice of problem-solving skills. Part 2 would focus on emotion-focused coping, including the A-B-C-D exercise.

## Homework Review

Review the homework from the last session—i.e., the helpful thoughts exercise, capturing cognitions exercise, Appraisal Worksheet, and continued practice with breathing exercises. It is often useful to start by having the client describe the homework assignment and rationale for assigning it. This is a fairly quick way to assess retention and understanding. Clarify and educate when needed. Identify any obstacles to completing the homework and problem solve as needed. Remind participants that homework is key to getting the most out of the program. True learning comes from repeated practice and application.

Most clients will have difficulty with the final step on the Appraisal Worksheet (i.e., rewriting the appraisals). Normalize their struggle and provide a few simple examples of rewritten appraisals if needed. Clients will get more practice in rewriting thoughts in this session's A-B-C-D exercise.

## Using Appraisals to Guide Coping

By now clients should have a fairly solid idea about the process of moving from experiencing a stressor to making appraisals to having stress symptoms (review Fig. 2.4 in Session 2). Today's session takes this one step further and focuses on how a person responds to or copes with stress. Explain that by coping we mean making the best response we can to any type of problem that comes our way.

The key to successful coping is being able to match the coping strategy with the needs of the stressful situation. The needs of the situation are usually determined by the details of the primary and secondary appraisals (i.e., specifics about the stressor and what needs to be done). Before selecting a coping strategy it is important to review the primary and secondary appraisals. Primary appraisals are about the nature and importance of the stressor; they will give us clues about what we can do to address the stressor. Secondary appraisals are about our coping abilities and resources. The Appraisal Worksheet (from Session 2) is a strategy to improve the accuracy and usefulness of appraisals. Once appraisals have been rewritten and improved, the stressor(s) should be broken down into more manageable components that can be prioritized and more easily analyzed for required coping strategies.

Examples of important questions to help break down and analyze appraisals are given below.

1. *What's the most important stressful situation (i.e., the main stressor)?*

   When multiple or chronic stressors are present, it is sometimes quite difficult to identify the main cause of stress. Clients may be aware of the physical sensation of stress or tension but be unaware of what is causing it. Give some examples of how a client can uncover the cause of a stressful feeling:
   - *What were you doing or thinking when the feeling started?*
   - *What thoughts or activities make the feeling stronger or weaker?*
   - *Have any new problems emerged or have chronic problems changed recently?*
   - *If you could magically erase one problem in your life to make it better, what would you pick?*

2. *What are the stressful elements of the situation and which elements are most important?*

   This step encourages the client to break a stressor down into more manageable, prioritized components that might require different coping strategies (a variant of "graded task assignments"). For example, an upcoming doctor's appointment might be causing a robust stress response. Elements of the stressor could include lack of transportation to the visit, uncertainty about how to prepare, fear of not remembering the doctor's instructions, dread of hearing bad news, the pain of walking up a flight of stairs to the doctor's office, etc. Each of these elements might require a very different coping strategy applied at a particular time.

3. *Are these elements changeable or unchangeable?*

   This step helps a client decide if he should roll up his sleeves and try to change something (i.e., problem-focused coping) or if he should practice acceptance and mood management (i.e., emotion-focused coping). In the above example of the doctor's office, finding transportation is something that is changeable and can be arranged ahead of time. Whether or not the doctor has bad news (such as bad lab results) is not changeable—i.e., it is not under the client's control, so efforts to force a change aren't likely to be helpful. Instead, the client should use emotion-focused coping. Most situations require a mixture of both problem-focused and emotion-focused coping but in different proportions at different times.

4. *Will this be a short-lived or chronic situation?*

   Chronic situations are generally less changeable and require a greater proportion of emotion-focused coping. Acute stressors may be novel and present special coping challenges. Thinking about duration helps one set more realistic expectations.

5. *What am I able to do now? Later? What about my family and friends?*

   After identifying and prioritizing the stressor elements, the client should revisit his secondary appraisals about his ability to cope and his available coping resources. By looking at more manageable pieces of the stressor, clients may see more opportunities for coping or ways in which others can help out.

## Example

Go over the following example with the client. All steps are covered for one stressor element (e.g., taking medications). Have the client go back and repeat the steps for the other stressor elements (e.g., having too many doctors appointments, uncontrolled pain, etc.)

*Jane is feeling extremely stressed about her health. She's taking loads of medications, seeing a half dozen doctors, and still feels very weak and in pain.*

1. What is the stressful situation?

   *Jane's continuing poor health.*

2. What are the stressful elements of the situation? Which are most important to her? (Ask Who? What? Where? When?)

   *She has to take loads of complicated medications every day that have side effects.*

   *She has many doctor's appointments every week.*

   *She feels weak, especially in the evenings.*

   *She has unrelieved physical pain especially when she sits upright or stands for too long.*

   *Her future is uncertain and she fears being helpless and in greater pain (most important).*

3. Are the stressful elements changeable or unchangeable?

   *For example, Jane cannot change the fact that she has to take medications and the routines are often quite complex. Some hassle seems inevitable. However, she can change the techniques she uses to remember taking them and she can discuss changing medications with her doctor. After Jane has addressed the things that can be changed about her medication she needs to address her feelings.*

4. Will this be a short-lived or chronic situation?

   *It appears that Jane will have to stay on medications, since her disease is not curable. Taking meds will be a "chronic situation." She may be able to simplify the regimen but she will have to work on accepting the continuing need for meds.*

5. What is Jane able to do now? Later? What about her family and friends?

   *Jane is able to call her doctor(s) to request a review of her medications. She can be very clear about her goal to reduce or combine the medications she is taking. She can change to a pharmacy that will fill her pillbox for her. She can ask her husband to help her with her medications. She can talk with her diabetic friend who seems to have a good system for medication management.*

Ask the client to work through some of the other stressful elements. List other examples of both problem-focused and emotion-focused coping. Remind clients that the choice of coping strategies assumes that Jane's appraisals are accurate and helpful. If they are not, these appraisals should be restructured first and then a coping strategy selected if still necessary.

## Summary of Using Appraisals to Guide Coping

Pulling together material from this session and Session 2, summarize the appraisals and coping steps as follows:

1. Identify the stressful situation.

2. Write, evaluate, and rewrite the primary appraisals.

3. Write, evaluate, and rewrite the secondary appraisals.

4. Break the stressor down into smaller, manageable pieces (the stressful elements) and prioritize them.

5. Decide whether these elements are changeable or unchangeable.

6. Match problem-solving coping strategies to changeable elements and emotion-focused coping to unchangeable elements.

More on problem-focused coping and emotion-focused coping follows.

Reiterate that problem-focused coping strives to improve those aspects of the situation (or stressor) that can be changed. Many of the common symptoms of serious illnesses (e.g., insomnia, pain, shortness of breath, depression) are changeable, although 100% relief might not be possible. Since many stressors are partly changeable, the client's challenge will be to determine which elements he should try to change and how many attempts he should make before moving to acceptance and emotion-focused coping. You may encourage clients to hope for the best but be prepared to accept the worst.

Problem-focused coping is often an iterative process similar to the steps found in problem-solving therapy, or PST (e.g., Arean, 2001; Nezu, 1986):

1. Get the right attitude

2. Define the problem and set your goal.

3. List your options.

4. Pick an option.

5. Put it into effect and check your progress.

You may want to use the following dialogue to begin your presentation of these steps:

> *When you are sick and stressed it is hard to manage all of your problems. Sometimes there are just so many problems it seems too hopeless or overwhelming. You don't know where to start. But by taking it one step at a time and reminding yourself how to tackle tricky problems, you can better cope with whatever hassles and bigger problems come along. By only trying to change things that can realistically be changed, you might save a lot of precious time and energy.*

## Step 1: Get the Right Attitude

Explain that the first step in solving a problem (i.e., stressor or stressor element) is recognizing it and believing we can do something about it. We will know when we are faced with a problem, because our bodies will tell us, either through stress, anger, depression, anxiety, or confusion. These feelings, like any other bodily sensation, should be considered signals telling us that we are facing a problem. When we notice that we are feeling an emotion, it is time to stop and think about what is going through our heads. What were we just doing? What were we thinking about?

Emphasize that it is important to have faith that we can solve the problem. When we are depressed, it is very common to feel hopeless. It seems there are no solutions to a problem. When we feel and think this way, we are less likely to want to solve our problems. Suggest to the client that he try using the "yes-but" approach to making thoughts more problem oriented.

### Example 1

Unhelpful attitude: *It's hopeless. I'll never be able to find a doctor who understands my illness.*

Yes-but approach: ***YES,*** *it is hard finding a good doctor,* ***BUT*** *there are hundreds of doctors in the area and I can ask my family or friends for their input and advice. I won't know until I try.*

### Example 2

Unhelpful attitude: *I can never remember what my doctor tells me in our visits. It's hopeless to think I am going to be able to do what she asks.*

Yes-but approach: ***YES,*** *I have had trouble remembering what my doctor tells me,* ***BUT*** *I can ask him to write it down, bring a tape recorder, or ask my friend to come to the appointment with me.*

## Step 2: Define the Problem and Set Your Goal

Emphasize that a problem defined is a problem half-solved. When we can figure out exactly what is causing us stress or getting in the way of meeting our goals, we are in much better shape to tackle the problems and come up with helpful solutions. When we are ready to work on a problem and we have the right attitude about solving it, then the next step is to define the problem.

### What Is the Problem?

The first thing to do is uncover all the elements of the problem or stressful situation. Tell the client that our best bet is to act like a good investigative reporter. Reporters are taught to get only the facts of a situation and to answer the following questions: who, what, where, when, and how? It is important to use concrete and specific terms when defining the problem. Warn clients to stay away from vague statements, interpretations, or judgments. Refer the client back to the example of Jane above. Jane started with a vague sense of distress about her chronic illness. She was then able to specify several problems that her illness was causing (e.g., taking too many meds).

### What Is Your Goal?

After we have figured out what the problem is, the next step is to determine our goal. A goal is the outcome we would like to see happen when we address the problem. Goals should also be specific and concrete. Another important aspect of defining our goal is to be realistic. While everyone would love to be miraculously cured overnight, it is not a very realistic goal. We need to make sure that the goal is something we can reach, so we aren't disappointed. While it is okay to aim for the stars, we need to think of the practical steps to get us there.

### What Are the Obstacles to Your Goal?

Once we have figured out the goal, the next step is to figure out what the obstacles are. Obstacles are the people, places, feelings, or other things that might make achieving our goal more difficult. Obstacles are important to define, as solutions will generally be based on how to overcome the obstacles. We should think about what happens when we try to cope with a stressor. Do we get anxious? Does someone interfere with us reaching our goal? Is the goal too unrealistic?

## Step 3: List Your Options

Once we have our problem, goals, and obstacles defined, we then have to come up with ideas to solve the problem. When we are depressed, afraid, or sick, this is very hard to do. Our thinking may be unbalanced, inflexible, and judgmental. We may be relying on unhelpful "habits of mind," such as selectively attending to past failures or fortune telling bad events. We may judge our ideas before we've had a chance to really consider them. We or someone else thinks of a possible solution and we think, "Yes, but. . . ." During this part of problem solving, the client is not allowed to discard any solution, no matter how silly he thinks it is. The goal here is to come up with as many possible solutions as we can, at least 10 of them.

## Step 4: Pick an Option

Once we have come up with a list of solutions, we decide which one to use first. No solution should be discarded completely, in case the one we chose does not work. Even if a chosen option fails, the client may have learned something important (i.e., what not to do). Although a client may feel discouraged or even hopeless, it is important to stress that we can't be certain that there is no way out until we have exhausted all of our options. A first solution can be selected by asking the following questions:

1. Does this meet my short-term goals?

2. Does this meet my long-term goals?

3. What kind of effect does this solution have on me? Does it help me, or does it create new problems for me?

4. What kind of effect does this solution have on others? Does it help them, or does it create new problems for them?

5. How likely am I to to be able to put this solution into effect?

6. How likely is it to work?

Once we do that for each solution, we must pick the solution for which the pros most outweigh the cons. In the end, it might take several solutions done concurrently to address all of the aspects of a given problem. Alternatively, as more is learned about the situation, the client might want to go back to the original list of options and add new ideas to try out.

## Step 5: Put It into Effect and Check Your Progress

Now that we have a plan for a solution, it has to be implemented. Only by trying it out can we assess its effectiveness. First, clients should pick a time and date to implement the solution. Any necessary people or resources should be rallied or put into action.

Once the solution has been implemented, the outcome should be evaluated. The client needs to assess why the solution worked or did not work. It is important for the client to answer the following questions:

1. What was the outcome?

2. Was the outcome better, as good, or worse than I expected?

3. Would I use the solution again?

4. What would I do differently? What does this say about my problem?

5. Did I gather more information that was useful in redefining the problem?

6. Can I now move on to another problem?

## Little Things Matter

As a final note about problem-focused coping, tell clients that acting to change even little things in a big, stressful situation can make a difference in how we feel. Use an example like the following to illustrate this point.

*For example, Valarie was very ill and declining rapidly. There was nothing she could do anymore to reduce her symptoms (unchangeable). However, she felt much better when she realized she could still ask for her favorite food, enjoy her comfortable "special" pillow, listen to her favorite music, or ask her husband for a massage.*

Emphasize that no situation is ever 100% unchangeable. Encourage clients to look for the small things they can do that might make a difference in their lives.

Worksheets for each of the problem-solving steps are included in the workbook. Help clients begin filling out the exercises—i.e., defining the problem, setting a preliminary goal, listing one or two options to get started. Remind clients that their earlier work on breaking stressors down into stressor elements will assist them in defining a specific, addressable problem. Remember that only changeable problems should be used for this exercise. Unchangeable problems will be addressed in the next section.

## Emotion-Focused Coping

Tell the client that we have to acknowledge that there are certain elements in nearly every stressful situation that we cannot change. It's important to work to change what is changeable, but then also work to cope with our feelings about what's not changeable. Give these examples:

- *You can't change your medical diagnosis.*

- *You can't change the fact that your illness sometimes causes fatigue and pain.*

- *You can't make your significant other a different person.*

## Strategies for Emotion-Focused Coping

Although we can't change some things, we can make ourselves feel better about them. The sessions on depression, anxiety, and anger will cover mood management strategies, many of which are examples of emotion-focused coping. Other strategies include the following:

- Seeking social support

- Talking on the phone

- Going out to dinner

- Reading

- Watching television

- Using the Internet

- Exercise

- Focusing on the positives

- Keeping a gratitude journal

- Listening to music

- Humor (films, cartoons, books, laughing)

- Medications

- Pets

- "Mall therapy" (shopping)

- Volunteer work

- Relaxation

- Art projects

- Writing stories

- Praying

Ask clients if there are there other emotion-focused coping strategies they'd like to add to the list. Stress that these strategies might not solve the problem but they can make us feel better emotionally. If we feel better emotionally, our thoughts and our behaviors may shift in more helpful directions (recall the feelings–thoughts–behavior triangle).

## Steps for Emotion-Focused Coping

The steps for emotion-focused coping are similar to those for problem-focused coping.

1. Get the right attitude ("I CAN affect my mood").

2. Define the problem and your goal (which is to feel better, enjoy yourself, or forget about your problem).

3. List your options (like those in the list of strategies above).

4. Pick an option.

5. Put it into effect and check your progress (i.e., the effect on your mood).

## Affirmation Exercise

Tell the client that a powerful way to affect our moods is to use affirmations—i.e., self-soothing, positive coping statements. Affirmations are brief, positive statements about ourselves or our environment that provide comfort or inspiration or stimulate thought. It is important to remember that many clients have been experiencing a gradual decline in abilities and appearance due to their illness. If this is a concern, clients should be directed to think of those aspects of themselves that are not dependent on their physical abilities. Start the following list of affirmations with the help of the client and write these on a flip chart:

■ Things I'm proud of:

■ Memories that make me smile:

■ Things I like about myself:

■ "Signature strengths" I still have regardless of my illness:

There are also a number of affirming and inspirational books on the market. You may want to recommend some of these (see Appendix for more information):

*Love, Medicine, and Miracles* by Bernie Siegel

*Kitchen Table Wisdom* by Rachel Remen

*Chicken Soup for the Soul: Stories to Open the Heart and Rekindle the Spirit* by Jack Canfield and Mark Victor Hansen

## A-B-C-D Exercise

Another very useful emotion-focused coping skill is cognitive restructuring. It may or may not change the situation (i.e., the stressor) but changing the way we think will almost certainly change the way we feel (i.e., emotion-focused coping). In the A-B-C-D exercise we simply add one extra step to the A-B-C's of cognitive therapy. *D* for "Dispute." While the A-B-C exercise helps us understand why we feel a particular way or choose a particular behavior (i.e., the consequences), the A-B-C-D exercise allows us to dispute beliefs and possibly change the emotional or behavioral consequences. You may use Figure 3.1 to demonstrate this process.

The easiest way to do an A-B-C-D exercise is to use the A-B-C-D Form in the workbook or divide a blank piece of paper (or flip chart) into quadrants using a "+" in the middle of the page. The top left quadrant is the Activating Event and the top right quadrant is the Consequences. Note that both are "above ground" (i.e., the horizontal line) and clearly observable. Beliefs are in the bottom left quadrant ("below ground") and will require some excavating. The Dispute box is in the bottom right adjacent to the belief box. The disputations should be in direct response to the beliefs that have been listed.

Although disputations can be challenging, clients should use what they have learned in Session 2 regarding balance, flexibility, judgment, and

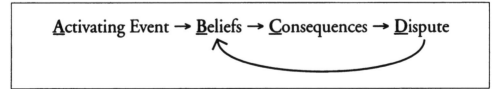

**Figure 3.1**
A-B-C-D Model

other habits of mind. The skills they have been learning on the rewriting of appraisals will also be applicable. You may instruct them to use the "yes-but" technique or some of the following strategies:

- What is the other side of the coin? Is there a middle ground?

- If your best friend had this thought, what would you say to support him or her?

- What is the evidence to support this thought? Is there evidence that argues against it?

- Check this opinion out with others. Do they see it the same way?

- Be sure to talk about behaviors and not character.

- Find the truth in what was said and learn from it. What can you do to solve this situation?

Share a completed A-B-C-D Form with the client before asking him to do one on his own (see example in the workbook). The client will also be asked to complete the A-B-C-D Form for homework and to evaluate the impact it had on his mood (i.e., its effectiveness as an emotion-focused coping strategy).

## Homework

- Have client complete the Coping Exercise in the workbook.

- Have client complete the Get the Right Attitude Worksheet.

- Have client complete the Problem Definition Worksheet.

- Have client complete the Set Goals and Identify Obstacles Worksheet.

- Have client complete the List Your Options Worksheet.

- Have client complete the Pick an Option Worksheet.

- Have client complete the Implementation and Evaluation Worksheet.

- Encourage client to use affirmations on a daily basis.

- Have client complete at least one A-B-C-D Form.

1. I am already doing all I can do to feel better. How do you expect me to do more?

   *A: There is no question that chronic illness places great demands on you. I am sure you are doing a great deal already to help yourself and your family. This program isn't necessarily about doing more. It is about working smarter rather than harder. It is intended to help you get to a better emotional place so that you have an easier time doing the things you have to do. The homework does take time, but we hope it is an investment that saves you time and energy later. Remember, too, that some of the homework isn't "work" at all. You may be asked to relax, to enjoy a movie, or tell a loved one you care.*

2. It isn't fair that I have to cope with so much while others have so little. Why should I have to do this? Why can't someone do it for me?

   *A: You are right. It is not fair that you are ill and have so much to cope with. It is hard to say why some have such heavy burdens to bear while others do not. Unfortunately, we play with the cards we are dealt. This program is intended to lighten your load. Later sessions will help you identify and recruit other supports that might be able to carry part of the load for you.*

3. Isn't emotion-focused coping a fancy term for denial? Avoidance? Being a "Pollyanna"?

   *A: Not really. It is a fact that there are some things that we simply cannot change. You cannot change your medical diagnosis. You cannot change your significant other's personality. Effective coping first requires us to separate things that are changeable from things that are not changeable. Emotion-focused coping is primarily used for things that are not changeable or whenever we need a brief break from what we've been doing. It doesn't "ignore" problems, it just acknowledges that efforts to change them may be futile. Instead of wasting time and energy, emotion-focused coping helps you accept a situation and improve your mood so you can cope with other problems.*

4. The disputes in the A-B-C-D model seem like clever ways to try to fool yourself. What if the beliefs are true to begin with? What if someone or something really is evil, bad, or unfair?

   *A: The disputes aren't about fooling yourself or playing "politician." The disputes are intended to help us see things in a more balanced and fair way. Since we all rely on habits of mind (or thinking short-cuts), we often make unfair judgments or come to biased conclusions. The dispute slows us down and asks us to reflect on our thinking. Some things may indeed be "bad, evil, or unfair." The dispute does not prevent us from acknowledging the truth. In those cases, it encourages us to learn from what has happened and think of a constructive response.*

5. How do I know when to do an A-B-C-D? What if I get stuck?

   *A: For your first few A-B-C-Ds, we recommend that you pick easier topics—i.e., topics that have a mild to moderate emotional charge or deal with daily hassles. What you pick is up to you, but try to fit in several per week if possible. Once you have learned how to do them, use your emotions as signals for when to do another one. In other words, if you start to feel angry or upset, consider doing an A-B-C-D about what just happened to cause that feeling. Don't worry if you get stuck. Everyone gets stuck at some point. Just bring your A-B-C-D Form to your next session and show it to your facilitator.*

# Module 2
## Mood Management

# Session 4 | *Illness and Mood: Depression*

*(Corresponds to session 4 of the workbook)*

## Materials Needed

- Flip chart or board
- My Signs and Symptoms of Depression form
- Emotion Detection and Filtering Worksheet
- Pleasant Activities List
- Activity Record and Scheduling Form

## Outline

- Set agenda
- Review homework
- Define and discuss depression
- Discuss medication as a treatment for depression
- Discuss therapy as a treatment for depression
- Discuss self-help as a treatment for depression
- Introduce activity monitoring and scheduling
- Introduce Pleasant Activities List
- Assign homework

## Setting the Agenda

Set the agenda by referring to the session outline. Ask the client if any other topics should be added. If an agenda list becomes too long, collaboratively prioritize the items. Given the amount of content in the last session, you may choose to reserve extra time to review the last session and go over the homework assignments.

## Homework Review

Review the homework from the last session with a special focus on the A-B-C-D exercise and steps in problem solving. For the A-B-C-D Form, most clients will find the Dispute box most difficult and will need some guidance in developing helpful disputations. It is probably wise to ask clients to do a second A-B-C-D Form either in session or as an additional homework assignment for the following week. The A-B-C-D exercise will be a useful strategy for all of the mood management sessions. Since the steps in problem solving will also be used in several future sessions, be sure that clients understand the process. If there were any obstacles to completing homework, use this as a new opportunity to practice the steps of problem solving outlined in the last session. If there were no obstacles to homework completion, be sure to practice problem solving with another recent issue. Remind the client that practice (i.e., homework) is key to getting the most out of the program.

## Definition of Depression

Discuss how being sick and stressed can have a very harmful effect on one's mood. The way we feel emotionally is greatly affected by how we feel physically. Both are affected by our thoughts and behaviors (refer to Figure 1.1 Mind-Body Medicine in Session 1 and Figure 2.1 Feelings–Thoughts–Behavior Triangle in Session 2). As a result, many people have to deal with being afraid and depressed on top of being physically ill. However, there are ways to effectively manage feelings of fear and depression. Today's session will focus on common symptoms, available treatments, and self-help for depression. Session 5 will address anxiety.

Explain that the term *depression* can refer to a brief feeling, a longer lasting mood, or a chronic medical disease. All of these instances of depression affect the way our bodies feel, how we think, and potentially how we behave.

Depression is normal as a feeling or mood. Everyone gets depressed, sad, or blue sometimes. Remind patients that feelings are ways to get our attention and provide important sources of information. The "information" (i.e., cognition, meaning, trigger) typically associated with depression has to do with loss. A feeling of depression often accompanies the perception of loss (e.g., of a loved one, a job, independence, appearance, income, health, etc.). Being chronically or terminally ill usually means temporarily or permanently losing a lot and having to adjust. In other words, being sick often means initially feeling depressed, having to accept one's losses, adapting to new circumstances, and moving onward. Some of the common losses that clients and their families may experience are listed in Table 4.1 below.

Sometimes it is too difficult to grieve these losses, accept them, and move onward. The depression may go from being a feeling or mood that conveys information to being a medical disease that can last for weeks, months, or even years. That condition may be associated with substantial fear, anger, and withdrawal—all normal and understandable responses to serious illness that will need to be managed (see later sessions).

Discuss with the client how a person knows if her depression is "normal" or is a medical condition. Although some of the interventions are similar for both cases, if depression is deemed a medical condition, then treatment is indicated.

### Table 4.1 Common Losses Caused by Serious Illness

| | |
|---|---|
| Physical strength and endurance | Employment |
| Income or financial assets | Body image and appearance |
| Loss of status, rank, or power | Control over one's own body |
| Control over the environment | Vision or hopes for the future |
| Functional ability (mobility, lifting, self-care) | Independence |

Go over the following warning signs (this brief list includes symptoms with the highest specificity and sensitivity):

1. You have had a low, sad, or depressed mood almost continuously for at least 2 weeks.

2. Your low mood impairs your ability to care for your health and/or accomplish your other everyday tasks.

3. Your low mood is beginning to negatively impact people around you and harm your social relationships.

4. You have been unable to enjoy things you usually enjoy for the past couple of weeks.

Other common symptoms include the following:

- Irritable mood

- Appetite or weight change (in either direction)

- Changes in how much you sleep (in either direction)

- Feeling tired all the time

- Changes in how you move (e.g., feeling jittery or slowed down)

- Poor concentration or poor memory

- Feeling worthless or guilty

- Thinking a lot about death, dying, or suicide

To be diagnosed with depression as a medical disease (i.e., major depression or clinical depression), remind clients that they must have five symptoms most of the day nearly every day for at least 2 weeks. Clients might want to circle the symptoms they have on the My Signs and Symptoms of Depression form in the workbook and discuss their severity and frequency. If clients meet diagnostic criteria, they should add major depression to their list of chronic diseases that should be a focus of treatment. It is important to note that there may be substantial overlap between the symptoms of clinical depression and the symptoms of the client's chronic disease—e.g., fatigue, insomnia, weight loss, etc. The emotional and cognitive symptoms of depression (e.g., low mood, anhedonia, hopelessness, guilt, suicidal ideation) are often weighted more heavily than the neurovegetative symptoms in this population. You many also use the results of the intake assessment to further corroborate a diagnosis of depression. Clients who meet diagnostic criteria should be engaged in developing a more focused and in-depth plan to treat their depression.

Although nearly all clients with serious illness will develop some depressive symptoms, only some will go on to develop the full-blown syndrome of major depression. It is believed that major depression is the consequence of systemic and chronic biological dysregulation triggered by losses such as those caused by serious illness. In the case of major depression, the body and mind are not able to reestablish balance and order following the stressor, hence the ongoing dysregulation of sleep, appetite, energy, and other bodily systems. Fortunately, balance can be reestablished, although clients may be more vulnerable to dysregulation in the future.

When depression is subsyndromal or a "normal" reaction to loss (i.e., not a medical condition) it doesn't necessarily require professional treatment. Participants may still find counseling helpful or could try some of the self-help suggestions in this program. Acknowledge that identifying losses, grieving, coping, and moving onward is hard and often painful work. Most of the sessions in the program are designed to help clients through this important process.

This session covers three categories of help for depression: medications, psychotherapy or counseling, and self-help. As clients learn about each option, the usefulness and goodness-of-fit based on client preferences and clinical need should be discussed. Clients who meet diagnostic criteria for depression need more focused and in-depth treatment—either additional sessions on stress and mood management, an adjunctive CBT depression protocol, or concurrent antidepressants.

## Antidepressant Medication

If the client has major depression, some portion of this session should be devoted to education about antidepressant medication and discussion of client preferences for treatment. If the client does not meet criteria for major depression, the coverage of this section can be abbreviated with more time spent on therapy and self-help options.

There are many effective antidepressant medications currently on the market. Most are covered by insurance and some are available as inexpensive generics. The newer drugs have fewer side effects and some have fewer drug–drug interactions (especially important for clients already on multiple medications for other diseases). If participants are interested in treating their depression with drugs, they should speak to their medical doctor. Some pointers on whether to consider meds and how to select a particular medication are discussed next.

## How Antidepressants Work

Briefly explain how antidepressants work. These medications help restore a natural balance to the chemicals in the brain that help create mood—just like insulin restores a natural balance to blood sugar in diabetics. In addition to restoring balance, these drugs improve the growth and functioning of neurons in the brain—much like vitamins and antioxidants improve the functioning of our cells or our immune system. These medications do not have to be taken permanently but may have to be taken for extended periods of time, depending on how well the person is doing. There are no antidepressants that are physically addictive, but clients might need to taper off the medications if they decide to stop them, rather than quitting abruptly.

Remind patients that they will have to take their antidepressant medication every day even if they aren't feeling depressed that day. Antidepressant medications need time to alter neuronal structure and function before they can have a therapeutic effect. They also need to stay at a certain level to remain effective. Although the chemical balance of the brain is quickly improved, it takes longer for the drugs to improve the growth and function of the neurons. Side effects may appear right away (e.g., drowsiness, dry mouth), but typically it takes 4–6 weeks before the medications begin to show a therapeutic effect. If a particular medication doesn't seem to help, a doctor can increase the dosage or prescribe a new medication.

## Choosing an Antidepressant

How can a client know which antidepressant is right for him? Unfortunately, there is currently no test that tells us who will respond to which antidepressant. Most choices are based on simple trial and error. Since it takes 4–6 weeks to know if a medication will work, it may take several months of trying different meds before finding the one that works. This process may be improved by having the client consider some of the following issues.

1. *Have you ever tried any antidepressants in the past? If so, what was the dose and duration of the trial? What were the side effects? Did it work for you?*

   Assist the client in writing down this information to take to the prescribing MD. Many clients will have tried antidepressants in the past; however, the dosage may not have been sufficient or the trial may have been too short for a therapeutic response. Any and all of these data will be helpful to the physician prescribing medication.

2. *What side effects are least desired? Are there any side effects that would be considered beneficial?* (e.g., drowsiness in a client with insomnia)

   All medications have the potential for side effects and antidepressants are no different. Selecting a medication may be based on its side effect profile.

3. *Do you have a biological family member who has responded well to an antidepressant?*

   Although this is not a guarantee that the client will also respond well, there is a greater chance due to pharmacogenetics (i.e., genes partly determine how we will metabolize and respond to certain meds).

4. *What does your insurance cover? If you are not insured, what is the cost of the medication?*

   A medication should not be started if continuing access will be problematic.

## Other Medications

It will be important to remind clients that a lack of response to one medication does not indicate a failure. There are multiple classes of medications that can be tried in addition to psychotherapy (discussed next). For some patients with serious and/or terminal illnesses, stimulants or anxiolytics (i.e., anxiety meds) are also used as adjunctive treatment for depression. While these classes of medications do not restore chemical balance or improve neuronal growth or function, they can provide some more immediate symptomatic relief. While both classes may carry the risk for addiction, many providers believe that risk is acceptable as a client enters the end of life. If substantial fatigue or agitation is present, the client may inquire about these as adjunctive treatments usually given along with an antidepressant.

## Adherence and Side Effects

After a medication(s) has been selected, it is important to monitor treatment response and promote adherence. Clients may want to take a depression symptom questionnaire (e.g., Beck Depression Inventory; see Assessment chapter for others) at the initiation of treatment to establish a baseline and repeat the measure over time. A simple check-in a few days after the client starts the medication can promote adherence by assuaging fears about side effects and brainstorming ways to remember to take the meds. If adherence is defined as a problem, then the problem-solving steps in Session 3 can be applied. The client may note certain side effects, but excessive side effect monitoring is not advised. It is important to remember that even sugar pill placebos are attributed with side effects, so some of the side effects initially experienced may fade over time. Other common side effects such as fatigue and gastrointestinal (GI) upset may diminish or can be easily managed (e.g., take pill before bedtime if fatigued, take pill with food if GI upset).

Fortunately, medications are not the only option for the treatment of major depression. Psychotherapy or professional counseling has also been shown to be effective. Unlike with medications, this category of interventions can also be helpful for clients with subsyndromal or "normal" depressive symptoms. Treatment can be both curative and growth oriented. There are many different theories about how or why therapy works, but the bottom line is that it works in both individual and group formats. Many people find therapy a helpful and acceptable alternative to medication. Others combine therapy and medication to get the most benefit. While this program can be considered therapy, it does not focus exclusively on the treatment of depression. Many of the skills, however, are taken from depression-specific treatments such as CBT.

## How Therapy Works

Explain that therapy can help people who are depressed change their thinking, their ways of coping, and their activities. Therapy can help resolve personal and family conflicts and make life transitions easier. Sometimes it helps just to have an impartial, supportive, and helpful person to talk to in a safe, confidential setting. Emphasize that being in therapy doesn't mean a person is crazy. When a client is newly diagnosed with diabetes, she should go to a diabetes class or counselor to learn how to manage diabetes. When a client is newly diagnosed with depression, it makes equal sense to go to a depression class or counselor to learn how to manage depression. Stress that it's wise for a person to get help when she needs it. Even if a client does not meet the criteria for major depression, the burden of coping with serious illness and stress can often be alleviated with supportive and skill-based therapies.

## Different Types of Therapy

There are many types of therapy and many therapists use a mixture of these types. If a client has been diagnosed with major depression, then the therapy prescribed should be one that has been empirically proven to work. If a client is seeking assistance with grief, coping, growth, or quality of life in general, there is wider latitude in selecting treatment options. The types of therapy proven to successfully treat depression include cognitive-behavioral therapy (CBT), interpersonal psychotherapy (IPT), and problem-solving therapy (PST). Cognitive-behavioral therapy includes changing negative thoughts and behaviors in order to feel better. Interpersonal psychotherapy focuses on the interpersonal context in which depression occurs and works to improve interpersonal relationships and ease transitions. Problem-solving therapy teaches a structured approach to identifying problems and goals then selecting and evaluating promising solutions (see Session 3).

This program uses a CBT approach and teaches stress management and problem-solving skills. Examples of CBT interventions in this program include capturing cognitions, challenging habits of mind, A-B-C-D exercises, structured approaches to coping, and relaxation strategies. CBT was selected because of its wide empirical support for alleviating the symptoms of stress, depression, and anxiety. The CBT structure and focus on skill-building also seemed to resonate most with the requirements of chronic disease self-management. By teaching clients exportable skills, it is hoped that they will eventually become their own expert therapist. If patients are interested in other types of therapy, you should assist them with referrals or have them speak with their physician about what types might be best for them.

## What to Expect

Almost any type of therapy requires patience and ongoing personal investment and work. If a person has major depression, she will most likely need at least 10–12 visits to make lasting progress, although even one visit can sometimes help a person feel temporarily better. Therapy typically starts with one or more intake sessions during which information is shared to make a diagnosis, decide upon a treatment, and set the goals of therapy. This is also the client's opportunity to interview the therapist and share any questions or concerns. Clients should be given a brief orientation to the therapist's practice or clinic. Consent to treatment should be obtained and should include information about confidentiality and client rights.

The sessions after the intake will vary widely depending on the type of therapy chosen. In general, the aim of therapy is to help patients learn new ways to manage their moods and the daily stresses in their lives so they can continue growing and changing even after the therapy is over. The process for achieving this aim might include guided exploration for insight, focusing on the relationship with the therapist, practicing new behavioral skills such as relaxation or activity scheduling (see page 91), and capturing and rewriting cognitions (see Sessions 2 and 3).

### "Side Effects" and Outcomes of Therapy

Emphasize that therapy doesn't work for everyone. Sometimes it can be difficult to talk about personal or painful issues or there might not be a good match between patient and therapist. Sometimes the goals set in therapy might be too unrealistic or the goals of the client may not match the goals of the therapist. It is also possible that escalating symptoms of physical illness might make attendance and participation in therapy quite difficult. Although some evidence suggests that therapeutic gains are long lasting, the progress can sometimes be slow and clients may feel worse before they feel better. Painful issues may need to be activated before they can be resolved.

If a therapy does not seem to be going well, the following guiding questions may be used to uncover and address the root cause.

- Does the client believe that therapy can help? Are serious doubts and excessive skepticism undermining therapy? Is the client able to temporarily suspend disbelief to give the treatment a fair shot?

- Do the client and therapist share the same goals? Do they agree on the methods that should be used to achieve those goals?

- Has the client's medical condition changed? Is there a new medical or psychiatric diagnosis that should be taken into consideration (e.g., substance abuse, recurrence of cancer)?

- Has a new stressor entered the client's life? Does the stressor alter the client's ability to participate in treatment? Does it alter the goals or necessary process?

- Is cultural, gender, age, or other differences between the client and therapist causing mistrust, misunderstanding, or miscommunication? Can these be resolved or should a better match be found?

- Does the type of therapy chosen match the needs of treatment? Is the therapy evidence based for that disorder in individuals similar to the client?

## Self-Help

While there is no "right" way to cope with subsyndromal or "normal" depression, strategies typically involve some mixture of self-help, social support, and counseling. Clients may first want to try the exercises included in this program. For additional exercises, they may try one of the self-help manuals available, such as *Feeling Good* by David Burns, and *Mind Over Mood* by Greenberger & Padesky. Other self-help strategies are listed next. While these strategies are labeled as self-help, clients may need initial guidance and support to learn and constructively use them.

## Develop Self-Awareness

Encourage the client to learn to identify and label important feelings as they occur. This skill involves the ability to both detect and filter emotions. *Detection* refers to the ability to know that an emotion is occurring. For most clients, the physiological changes associated with an emotion are easiest to notice. *Filtering* refers to the ability to decide which emotions should be attended to and which emotions can be left alone. Refer clients to the Emotion Detection and Filtering Worksheet in the workbook. Clients should write down idiosyncratic ways of detecting when they are feeling sad or depressed. To facilitate filtering, have clients begin a list of guidelines that help them decide when to invest the time to understand and perhaps change a particular emotion. For example, filters may be based on intensity of emotion (i.e., strong emotions get attention first), novelty (i.e., new emotions may be important to explore), duration (e.g., transient blips may not be worth worrying about), triggers (e.g., emotions triggered by marital conflict get high priority), or current energy or ability levels (e.g., processing emotions is typically not a good idea when exhausted or in pain).

The identified and labeled important emotions should then be understood as much as possible. Clients should try asking themselves, "Why do I feel this way right at this moment?" Feelings can be important sources of information that tell us something about ourselves, our relationships, or our world. Facilitate discussion by asking clients when they feel most depressed and most happy. Have them describe what they are thinking and doing at these times. What are the interrelationships between feelings, thoughts, and behaviors? Use the A-B-Cs of cognitive therapy to highlight this point (see Session 2).

By improving self-awareness, clients will have greater understanding and more control over their feelings. Once a feeling has been detected and understood, the client can choose from a long list of menu options to best manage that feeling. For example, if a feeling arises from cognitive imbalance or error, the client can do an A-B-C-D exercise (see Session 3). If the feeling reflects an accurate perception of an unchangeable situation, the client can try interventions to lift her mood (see Emotion-Focused Coping in Session 3).

## Acknowledge and Grieve Losses

Recall that depression often reflects the perception of loss. Being ill may mean that some very distressing and uncontrollable changes are occurring in the client's life or body. Normalize feelings of loss and sadness. Let clients know that it's okay to cry (or rage) alone or with friends and family. It is healthy to recognize and express their grief in whatever way they are able. As clients may know, grief often waxes and wanes over time. Grief may come in waves, causing a client to feel overwhelmed one day but relatively stable and accepting the next. It is important for clients to acknowledge their losses and the meaning of those losses. Losses often include the fear of continuing loss and growing dependence. While some clients will see losses as proof that they will become an unbearable burden on their loved ones, others fear loss because they believe it will render them unlovable or beyond support. Although these losses may be irreversible, mood can be improved by reinforcing important relationships, recognizing and savoring things not lost, or using other coping strategies such as cognitive restructuring or activity scheduling.

## Work for Mental Balance

As with stress, "normal" depression can be worsened by unhelpful ways of thinking. When losses are recent or have special significance, they often loom large and seem insurmountable. Ask the client to identify some of the valuable things she still has in her life. This strategy is not meant to deny or diminish the importance of the losses that have occurred. It is intended to help clients achieve better balance by acknowledging both losses and assets. You may want to use the following questions to facilitate discussion of current positives or gains:

▨ *What makes you look forward to the future?*

▨ *What things make you feel grateful?*

▨ *Has this illness helped you reorder your priorities? What are your priorities?*

▨ *Has this illness brought others closer to you?*

▨ *Has this illness caused you to change in any positive way?*

▨ *Has it made you more spiritual?*

▨ *What are other good things going on in your life that are separate from this illness?*

Since much of the perception of loss involves remembrance of the past or the way things used to be, it is important to strive for balance when thinking about the past. It is easy to idealize things that have been lost and to forget things that were permanently gained. The following questions might help clients work toward balance in thinking about the past.

▨ *What was the downside of working full time at full effort? Now that you can no longer work, is there something to be gained in this transition?*

- *How close were you to your family and friends when you were "fully functional?" Has this illness moved any obstacles out of the way of intimacy?*

- *Were you ever depressed, anxious, or stressed when you didn't have this serious medical condition? Was life really as good as you remember? What were the highs and the lows? If there can be lows when you were healthy, can't there be highs when you are sick?*

- *What were some of your biggest lifetime accomplishments that will survive you? What is your legacy? What makes you proud?*

## Be Goal Directed

Emphasize that it always helps to have something to look forward to, whether it's a trip, an anniversary, or something much smaller. In Session 10, the client will spend more time on setting goals and looking forward. For now, ask the client to recall the initial goals set in Session 1. Are these goals still relevant? Has the client made any progress toward these goals? Ask the client to consider any steps she can take toward achieving these goals. If new goals have emerged, have the client add them to the Goals Form (Session 1) or in the spaces provided in Session 5.

## Activity Monitoring and Scheduling

Activities (or behaviors) are closely related to mood. When an individual is depressed, she is usually less active, which makes her more depressed, which makes her less active, and so on (a classic downward spiral). Activity monitoring is a way to assess both quantity and quality of activities in a client's life. Activity scheduling is a method used to mindfully change the type or number of activities chosen. By changing activities, one hopes to see a corresponding change in mood.

## Activity Monitoring

Remind clients that they have already been practicing the important skill of self-monitoring. They have been monitoring their cognitions, appraisals, and solution outcomes. They have been considering how thoughts affect mood and behavior. By paying careful attention to what they think, do, or feel, clients have more personally relevant "data" to use when making choices about how to best improve their quality of life.

With activity monitoring, clients should direct their attention to their daily activities or behaviors. These activities include things the client has to do (e.g., chores, appointments) and things the client wants to do (e.g., talking with a friend, eating out). A comprehensive record of activities helps the client uncover patterns in both activity levels and types of activities that are chosen. The client may discover that evenings and weekends tend to have unstructured time (and consequent boredom or low mood). Clients may also discover that their days are filled with chores but little time is taken for enjoyment or stress reduction.

Introduce the Activity Record and Scheduling Form in the workbook. Explain that it can be used to monitor (i.e., record) current activities and/or to schedule future activities. Monitoring current activities can help participants identify open periods of time or periods of low mood that need to be filled with enjoyable activities. Have clients fill out what they have done thus far today before and up to this session. Ask them to begin recording daily activities for the next week. To assess the hypothesized relationship between higher activities levels and mood, clients should also rate their mood at the end of each day on a simple 1–10 scale.

## Activity Scheduling

With activity scheduling, clients make a conscious effort to either balance out their activity choices or fill the typical empty times in the week with uplifting activities. It is important for clients to have a "healthy" diet of activities—i.e., a balanced mixture that gives a sense of accomplishment and pleasure, social contact and solitude, relaxation and stimulation, comfort and challenge, etc. The key is helping clients see that they have activity choices and select activities that will have maximum mood impact.

Scheduling pleasant activities is an effective yet simple mood management strategy. While illness may limit or prevent certain activities, there are many things clients can still do that can help them enjoy their days and feel less depressed. Most clients will have many "have-tos" in their week but few "want-tos." Discuss the importance of scheduling pleasant activities (i.e., "want-tos"), just as we schedule other required activities. You may want to use the following dialogue:

*Sometimes the "have-tos" take up all your time so you can't do the "want-tos." You have to go to a doctor's appointment but you want to read a good book. Why not make an appointment with yourself or a friend to do a pleasant activity? One of your many "jobs" is to manage your disease and the stress or depression that comes along with it. Part of that management includes scheduling time for activities that will help you feel better. It is not about self-indulgence. It is about effective mood management. Pleasant activities are part of your treatment too!*

## Common Obstacles

Setbacks are common, as are obstacles to changing behavioral habits. Review common obstacles that might emerge when clients begin to consider adding new activities to their week.

- Too tired or sick

- Not enough money

- No transportation

- No activities companion

- Can't think of anything to do

- Not enough time

- No motivation

- Bad weather

- Seems like a big hassle

Discuss with the client if any of these apply to her. When selecting activities to schedule (from the Pleasant Activities List below), advise her to select activities that circumvent these obstacles and help her use problem solving to move past these obstacles. You may need to encourage her to "suspend disbelief"—i.e., put her prediction that it won't work aside for now and try it anyway to see what happens.

## Pleasant Activities List

Introduce the Pleasant Activities List (refer to the workbook). This incomplete list includes a wide range of activities, some of which take very little energy and no money, and require no transportation or companionship. A broad range is provided since some activities may appeal to some clients but may not appeal to others. Encourage clients to have an open mind and to circle a few activities to schedule for the next week. They may also choose to write in pleasant activities not listed. By doing these activities, they will be able to test the idea that doing enjoyable things will improve their mood.

After clients have circled a few pleasant activities, ask them to return to the Activity Record and Scheduling Form. In addition to recording the activities they do throughout the next week, they should use the form to prospectively schedule in their selected items from the Pleasant Activities List (recommend that scheduled activities be written in pencil so clients can erase or move them if needed). Clients are free to also schedule "have-to" activities (e.g., filling out health insurance paperwork, making a doctor's appointment) if this seems like the most effective mood management activity. While "have-tos" are not necessarily enjoyable, they do impart a sense of accomplishment and achievement. To create a "success" experience, it is important for clients not to overreach and schedule too many activities. Discuss how realistic their selected activities might be and recalibrate if needed. Have clients schedule in at least one or two activities while in session.

One common question clients ask is whether they should just rest until they feel better. The answer is yes and no. Yes, patients should respect their physical limits and take time to rest and recharge. However, being sick does not mean having to be bored and inactive all the time. Even in low-energy or impaired-mobility periods, clients can still choose from a menu of low-demand activities (e.g., reading a book, watching a movie, taking a bath, listening to music). Clients may also assume that they need to feel motivated to do something before doing it. However, if they wait around to feel motivated they may never do anything. Remind clients that action sometimes precedes motivation—i.e., once they get started doing something they will start to get into it and feel more motivated.

## Homework

✎ Have client complete My Signs and Symptoms of Depression form.

✎ Have client make a plan for treating her depression, if relevant.

✎ Have client complete the Emotion Detection and Filtering Worksheet.

✎ Have client answer questions in the Self-Help section of the workbook and try strategies.

✎ Have client review the Pleasant Activities List in the workbook.

✎ Have client use the Activity Record and Scheduling Form to monitor activities and schedule at least one or two new pleasant activities.

## FAQs from Clients

1. How is doing "pleasant" things supposed to cure my depression? You told me depression was a medical condition. Can the "cure" be that simple?

   *A: It is important to remember that pleasant activity scheduling is just one of the early strategies used in a typical course of a cognitive-behavioral therapy. Treatment that focuses on depression would include much more. However, it is important not to discount the power of activity scheduling—there is more to it than meets the eye. Pleasant activities are about enjoyment but they also require motivation, planning, control, hope, and sometimes contact with social supports. And don't forget that a lot of little activities can sometimes add up to a big mood impact. Just think of how worn down you can get from a lot of little daily hassles. It can work in the positive direction too!*

2. We're only in Session 4 and I am way behind in my homework. This is moving too fast for me. I'll never catch up. Help!

   *A: You're right. We have covered a lot of material in just a few weeks, but the pace lightens up from here on out. The second and third sessions are probably the most packed of the whole program. We will keep coming back to capturing thoughts, A-B-C-D exercises, and problem solving in nearly every session, so you will have many more opportunities to practice. If you still feel lost, we can always add in an extra session or two and help you catch up.*

3. I hear what you're saying about coping with mood, but my main problem is other people. I would be fine if my family weren't so difficult or if people would just leave me alone. My feeling bad is not my fault!

   *A: I'm sorry you are having trouble with other people. It's true that the people around us can greatly influence the way we feel. In Sessions 7 and 8 we will spend a lot of time talking about social supports and conflict resolution. For now, though, I recommend that we focus on the person who is most under your control—and that's you. We all have a choice in how we think about and behave towards other people. You should make sure that the interpersonal choices you are making are best suited to your goals. And don't forget that stress and depression make a lot of people crawl into a cocoon, even if it would help them to reach out more. Let's be sure that isn't the case for you.*

# Session 5 | *Illness and Mood: Anxiety*

*(Corresponds to session 5 of the workbook)*

## Materials Needed

- Flip chart or board
- My Symptoms of Anxiety form
- My Mental Hygiene Program form

## Outline

- Set agenda
- Review homework
- Define anxiety and review common symptoms
- Introduce steps for dealing with anxiety
- Discuss self-help as a treatment for anxiety
- Conduct diaphragmatic breathing
- Conduct progressive muscle relaxation and/or guided imagery
- Discuss medication as a treatment for anxiety
- Discuss therapy as a treatment for anxiety
- Review steps for dealing with anxiety
- Assign homework

## Setting the Agenda

Set the agenda by referring to the session outline. Ask the client if any other topics should be added. If the agenda becomes too long, collaboratively prioritize the items.

## Homework Review

Review the homework from the last session. If the homework was completed, clients will have daily mood ratings and a record of their activities from the past week, including the one or more pleasant activities they tried to add. Look at the Activity Record and Schedule together to identify any notable phenomena—e.g., periods of open time, busy times, highest mood day, lowest mood day, etc. Have clients consider how activity levels affected mood (e.g., was mood highest on the busiest day and lowest on the most inactive day?). What activities were most potent in terms of affecting mood in either a positive or negative direction? Was the client able to do the one scheduled pleasant activity? Why or why not? What mood impact did it have? Would scheduling more pleasant activities be helpful? Have the client consider any future activity goals.

If the homework was not completed, identify any obstacles to completing the homework and problem solve as needed. Collaboratively fill out a few cells on the activity schedule, starting with activities on the day of this appointment (e.g., "When did you get up? What did you do this morning? What will you do after this appointment?"). Fill in the highlights of the past week including any pleasant activities. With these limited data, see if the client can see a relationship between activities and mood. Elicit client agreement to keep an activity schedule in the following week.

## Definition of Anxiety

Begin the discussion by normalizing the fears that illness, disability, and death often bring. Everyone feels some anxiety sometimes, and people who are seriously ill may feel a lot of anxiety a lot of the time. However, anxiety isn't necessarily a foe to be beaten. We may feel anxious for a reason. Anxiety can help us feel aroused and ready to face a challenge; however, when unnecessary or excessive, it can leave us paralyzed with fear. Just like with depression, we need to monitor and understand our level of anxiety and what's causing it. This session continues our deeper look at mood management by including tips for coping with anxiety effectively.

By *anxiety* we simply mean feeling nervous, worried, troubled, uneasy, stressed out, or fearful. Anxiety can refer to an emotion, a physical state, and a frame of mind. The feeling of being stressed out often includes a fairly large component of anxiety. Whereas depression is about the perception of loss, anxiety is about the perception of danger coupled with doubts about one's ability to cope. In other words, there is a threat looming on the horizon and the person is not sure if he can handle it effectively.

## Capturing the Symptoms of Anxiety

Explain that our bodies respond to stressors by making us tense and alert so we're ready to face the problem. This is called the "fight-or-flight" response because, in addition to being a signal, it prepares us to either fight an attack or flee from the threat. This system works well unless we have a false alarm and there's really no threat. It can also be unhelpful when we have to face a problem that can't be directly fought or avoided. This system was designed to address short-term, changeable stressors. When the problem is chronic or unchangeable, the flight-or-flight response can do more harm than good.

Because of the large range of ways in which anxiety can manifest, it may be mistaken for other medical disorders. Common anxiety symptoms include the following:

- Excessive worry

- Difficulty concentrating

- Restlessness

- Fatigue

- Irritability

- Muscle tension

- Tension headaches

- Trouble sleeping

- Feeling jumpy or keyed up

- Feeling dizzy or light-headed

- Trembling

- Difficulty breathing

- Sweating (not due to heat)

- Numbness or tingling

- Heart racing

- Stomachache

- Withdrawal or avoidance

- Catastrophic or "doomsday" thoughts

- Panic attacks

Have the client review this list and discuss the frequency and intensity of relevant symptoms. Compare these results with the initial data collected during the intake. As with depression, it is important to remember that there may be substantial overlap between symptoms of anxiety and symptoms due to the client's medical disease or medications. Regardless of cause, however, if the client's symptoms have persisted for longer than a few days or if they cause social or occupational impairment, then anxiety management and/or a change in the treatment of the primary medical disease should be considered.

Like depression, anxiety can be an understandable response to stress, but it can also progress to a medical disease. If severity or chronicity suggests a DSM-IV-TR anxiety disorder (e.g., posttraumatic stress disorder [PTSD], panic disorder), then a careful diagnostic workup should be done. Therapy and medication options for both anxiety symptoms and full-blown anxiety disorders are discussed later in this chapter. It is important to remember that some clients may have experienced trauma as a consequence of their disease or treatment—e.g., having a heart attack, receiving aggressive chemotherapy, etc. If a client demonstrates symptoms of PTSD, he should be encouraged to consider cognitive-reprocessing and stress management therapies (see Therapy and Counseling section) and support groups.

## Dealing with Anxiety

Introduce the following steps for addressing symptoms of anxiety:

Step 1: Identify the cause(s) of your anxiety.

Step 2: Choose an intervention that addresses the root problem and/or the symptoms.

Step 3: Adopt new mental health habits to minimize future anxiety.

Discuss each step in detail with the client as follows.

## Step 1: Identify the Cause(s) of Your Anxiety

You may want to use the following dialogue to introduce this step:

> *Think of emotions as internal flare guns that go off to grab our attention. They often say, "Hey, wake up! Something's wrong! Pay attention!" In this way, emotions can be useful, but we have to be able to read and respond to the signal. When we feel anxious it is often our mind's way of telling us there's some potential threat or danger on the horizon that we might not be able to easily handle. We feel anxious and worry about the bills coming up, the next medical procedure, or what death might be like. That worry is meant to help us prepare. It is our job to receive the message, decide if it is a valid worry, then do something about it.*

To decide if we should heed this warning signal and what we might need to do, we first must identify and understand what is making us anxious. Often it is the ambiguity or newness of a situation that causes the most anxiety. Learning more about the cause of anxiety provides important information on how to cope in addition to providing a sense of control and empowerment. The following questions can help clients identify and understand the sources of their anxiety:

- *When you first started having these anxious feelings, what was going through your mind?*

- *Are there particular times, places, or people that create these anxious feelings within you?*

- *What things do you usually worry about?*

- *What scares you the most?*

- *Are there particular images, memories, or thoughts about the past or future that make you feel anxious?*

- *Why do you think these things bother you? What might they mean?*

- *Do these worries remind you of anything in your past?*

Since many anxieties may be tied to the client's serious illness, more illness-specific prompts might be helpful.

- *What scares you most about your illness?*

- *What illness-related symptoms cause the most fear?*

- *What do you fear the most when you think about your illness getting worse?*

- *What scares you the most about dying?*

- *Do these worries touch on any family memories of illness or death?*

## Step 2: Choose an Intervention

The next step is to select an intervention that addresses the cause and symptoms of anxiety. Once we have been able to identify the cause, the first task is to figure out if there is anything practical we can do to resolve it (i.e., problem-focused coping from Session 3). For example, if the problem is lack of money, are there other resources the client can tap into? If the cause is a new medical symptom, can the client talk with a physician? Remind participants that anxiety is a warning signal that tells us to pay attention to a problem and perhaps do something about it. Questions to ask include the following:

- *Are there any immediate steps you can take to change the situation or at least learn more about it?*

- *Are there people who can help?*

- *What resources are available to you?*

Encourage participants to use the problem-solving steps from Session 3. They may also consider using "graded task assignments" (in Session 3) or breaking a large stressor down into more manageable elements that can be addressed one at a time. This active approach to anxiety management has the potential to directly address the threat in addition to building clients' confidence in their ability to cope. Encourage clients to also use their social supports and medical team when facing problems. (Identification and utilization of social supports is covered in Session 7.)

If a client hasn't been able to identify and solve the cause of anxiety, residual anxiety symptoms could remain. There are several interventions that can provide some symptomatic relief. Since these interventions treat only the symptoms, they won't help solve the root of the problem. However, these treatments may put clients in a better frame of mind to think of ways to solve the problems later. These types of interventions include self-help, medications, and psychotherapy or counseling. Each of these will be discussed in turn below with opportunities for in-session practice. These interventions should be considered for immediate symptomatic relief and potentially as part of an ongoing anxiety management program.

## Step 3: Adopt New Mental Health Habits

While Step 2 assists clients in managing the anxiety symptoms of the moment, Step 3 encourages clients to develop regular habits of "mental hygiene" to prevent recurrence and improve anxiety management skills. Mental health habits are daily routines or activities that help keep the mind and emotions free of unnecessary clutter or generally keep levels of arousal low. Clients should draw heavily on newly developed skills of self-monitoring, cognitive balance, improving stressor appraisals, problem solving, emotion-focused coping, and somatic quieting (i.e., relaxation). For clients with more substantial anxiety symptoms, good mental health habits might include psychopharmacology and ongoing therapy. At the end of this session, clients will begin developing their mental hygiene plan for the upcoming months.

## Self-Help

Tell clients that there are many skills they can learn that can help them relax and cope with their anxiety more effectively. In this session we discuss and practice some of these techniques and will add new ideas in sessions to come. Remind clients that they have already been introduced to diaphragmatic (belly) breathing, balanced thinking, cognitive restructuring (A-B-C-D), problem solving, and activity scheduling. Although these interventions were introduced for stress and depression, they may work equally well for anxiety. Diaphragmatic breathing, progressive muscle relaxation, and guided imagery are presented here, although time may permit demonstration of only one or two of these interventions during the session. Remind clients that in addition to structured exercises, making minor changes to their environments can often reduce tension and anxiety—e.g., playing soft music, using aromatherapy, adjusting the lighting or temperature, etc. You may also want to recommend the following self-help books (see Appendix for more information):

*The Relaxation and Stress Reduction Workbook* by Martha Davis, Elizabeth Eshelman, and Matthew McKay

*The Anxiety and Phobia Workbook* by Edmund Bourne

*The PTSD Workbook: Simple, Effective Techniques for Overcoming Traumatic Stress Symptoms* by Mary Beth Williams and Soili Poijula

*An End to Panic: Breakthrough Techniques for Overcoming Panic Disorder* by Elke Zuercher-White

## Somatic Quieting

Remind clients of the brief discussion of somatic quieting (i.e., relaxation) at the end of Session 1. This category of interventions simply refers to techniques used to evoke a relaxation response—i.e., lower heart rate, blood pressure, decreased muscle tension, etc. (see Benson & Klipper, 2000). The relaxation response can be seen as the near opposite of the fight-or-flight response. Examples of somatic quieting exercises include diaphragmatic breathing, progressive muscle relaxation, meditation, yoga, guided imagery, Tai Chi, etc. The client may want to sample a variety of methods before selecting a regular practice. Once selected, this practice should be incorporated into the client's regular schedule.

## Diaphragmatic Breathing

Tell the client that a good place to start the fight against anxiety is with his breathing. When we get nervous, our breathing changes; it often gets shallow or rapid and some people even hold their breath. Unfortunately, these automatic responses only make anxiety symptoms worse. When the client notices anxiety, the first thing to think is "Breathe!" and try to keep breathing as slowly and deeply as possible. Remind participants that the best breaths come from the belly (i.e., using the diaphragm). Refer to the breathing exercise at the end of Session 1. If necessary, demonstrate diaphragmatic breathing again and explain why it has a calming effect.

## Progressive Muscle Relaxation

Recognizing and reversing muscle tension is another method for dealing with anxiety. Explain to the client that a common response to feeling nervous or worried is to tense the muscles in the neck, back, shoulders, or other areas of the body. Sometimes we're so used to tensing up that we don't even realize that we're doing it. One way to relax the mind is to relax the body. We can do that by systematically focusing on each muscle group in our body and trying to relax it. This is called "progressive muscle relaxation," or PMR.

Before beginning the PMR exercise, point out the eight muscle groups to be used. Tell the client that he will focus his attention on the specified muscle group and will then be asked to alternatively tense and relax it. The client should be careful not to tense too hard. If at any point the client feels pain or cramping, he should release his muscles immediately and tense less the next time. Each muscle group should be practiced twice in a row. End the exercise with whole body relaxation.

Use the following scripts for each muscle group. Pause 10 seconds as the client holds the tension. After the client releases the tension, pause another 10 seconds while he breathes and relaxes.

## 1. Arms

*Build up the tension in your arms by first putting your arms straight down and pressing them into your sides. Make a tight fist with each hand and curl your forearms upward. Imagine you are holding a very heavy box in your arms. Remember to keep making fists and press your elbows into your sides. Notice the sensations of pulling, discomfort, and tightness in your hands, lower arms, and upper arms. Hold the tension.* [Pause 10 seconds.] *Now release the tension and let your arms and hands relax, with palms facing down. Focus your attention on the sensations of relaxation through your hands, lower arms, and upper arms. As you relax, breathe smoothly and slowly from your abdomen. Each time you exhale, think "relax, relax, relax." Notice the difference between the sensation of tension and the feeling of relaxation.* [Pause 10 seconds.]

## 2. Legs

*Now, build up the tension in your legs by flexing your feet and pulling your toes toward your upper body, while pulling your knees together and lifting your legs off the floor. Feel the tension as it moves up your feet into your ankles, shins, calves, and thighs. Feel the pulling sensations from the hip down. Hold the tension.* [Pause 10 seconds.] *Now, release the tension, lowering your legs and relaxing the feet. Feel the warmth and heaviness of relaxation through your feet, lower legs, and upper legs. As you breathe smoothly and slowly, think the word "relax, relax, relax" each time you exhale.* [Pause 10 seconds.]

### 3. Stomach

*Now, build up the tension in your stomach by pulling your stomach in toward your spine very tightly. Feel the tightness. Focus on that part of your body and hold the tension.* [Pause 10 seconds.] *Now, let your stomach relax outward. Let it go further and further. Feel the sense of warmth circulating across your stomach. Feel the comfort of relaxation. As you breathe smoothly and slowly, think the word "relax" each time you exhale.* [Pause 10 seconds.]

### 4. Chest

*Now, build up the tension around your chest by taking a deep breath and holding it. Your chest is expanded, and the muscles are stretched around it. Feel the tension in your chest and back. Hold your breath.* [Pause 10 seconds.] *Now, slowly, let the air escape and breathe normally, letting the air flow in and out smoothly and easily. Feel the difference as the muscles relax, compared with the tension, and think the word "relax" each time you exhale. Notice the difference between the sensations of tension and the feeling of relaxation.* [Pause 10 seconds.]

### 5. Shoulders

*Imagine that your shoulders are on strings and are pulled up toward your ears. Feel the tension around your shoulders, radiating down into your back and up into your neck and the back of your head. Concentrate on the sensation of tension in this part of your body.* [Pause 10 seconds.] *Now let your shoulders droop. Relax and let them droop further and further. Focus on the sense of relaxation around your neck and shoulders. Feel the difference in these muscles from the tension. As you breathe smoothly and slowly, think the word "relax" each time you exhale.* [Pause 10 seconds.]

## 6. Neck

*Build up the tension around your neck by pressing the neck back and pulling your chin down toward your chest. Feel the tightness around the back of your neck spreading up into the back of your head. Focus on the tension.* [Pause 10 seconds.] *Now, release the tension, letting your head rest comfortably. Concentrate on the relaxation. Feel the difference from the tension. As you breathe smoothly and slowly, think the word "relax" each time you exhale.* [Pause 10 seconds.]

## 7. Mouth, Jaw, and Throat

*Build up the tension around your mouth, jaw, and throat by clenching your teeth and forcing the corners of your mouth back into a forced smile. Feel the tightness, and concentrate on the sensations of tension.* [Pause 10 seconds.] *Then, release the tension, letting your mouth drop open and the muscles around your throat and jaw relax. Concentrate on the difference in the sensations in that part of your body. As you breathe smoothly and slowly, think the word "relax" each time you exhale.* [Pause 10 seconds.]

## 8. Eyes and Forehead

*Squeeze your eyes tightly shut while pulling your eyebrows down and toward the center. Feel the tension across your lower forehead and around the eyes. Concentrate on the tension.* [Pause 10 seconds.] *Now release, letting the tension around your eyes slide away. Relax the forehead, smoothing out the wrinkles. Feel the difference of relaxation in comparison to tension. As you breathe smoothly and slowly, think the word "relax" each time you exhale.* [Pause 10 seconds.]

## Whole Body Relaxation

*Now your whole body is feeling relaxed and comfortable. As you feel yourself becoming even more relaxed, we'll count from 1 to 5. One, letting all of the tension leave your body. Two, sinking further and further into relax-*

*ation. Three, feeling more and more relaxed. Four, feeling very relaxed. Five, feeling deeply relaxed. As you spend a few minutes in this relaxed state, think about your breathing. Feel the cool air as you breathe in and the warm air as you breathe out. Your breathing is slow and regular. Each time you breathe out, think the word "relax." [Pause 10 seconds.] Now, count backward from 5, gradually feeling yourself become more alert and awake. Five, feeling more awake. Four, coming out of relaxation. Three, feeling more alert. Two, opening your eyes. One, sitting up.*

## Guided Imagery

Guided imagery offers a combination of relaxation and guided cognition to reach deeper levels of the relaxation response. Clients should first complete either the standard diaphragmatic breathing exercise or the PMR exercise. After clients have achieved a relaxed state, they should be guided in the process of creating self-soothing and inspirational cognitions to further immerse themselves in the experience and heighten mood management. Since many clients will have serious medical symptoms, it may be most helpful to guide them away from a focus on their disease. Something like the following may be used:

*Now that you have reached a state of relaxation through breathing (or PMR), continue to breathe in deeply and continue to feel to your muscles relaxing, relaxing, relaxing. With each exhale, imagine the tension leaving your body to be replaced with a sense of calm and wellness. Continue to breathe and continue to relax . . . Begin to create a mental image of the most peaceful place you can imagine. This place can be whatever and wherever you'd like it to be. Infuse it with a sense of calm, a sense of safety, and a sense of peaceful joy. Look around this place and notice what you see. Notice objects both near and far. You may be indoors or you may be outdoors. It is your place to create however you'd like. Notice any sounds, any smells, any tastes. Notice the temperature. It may be warm or it may be cool. Just continue to breathe in and relax and imagine your place of refuge. Notice how good your body feels in this peaceful place. You feel relaxed, at ease, free from pain, and free from worry. You may be alone or you may be with others. This is your world, your refuge, your place for comfort. Just continue to breathe, continue to drink in your surroundings, continue to enjoy the place you've created. . . . Take a last look around at this paradise you've created and remember that it is yours to return to anytime you want. Anytime, anywhere, your sanctuary awaits you. Just continue to breathe in and relax . . . On the count of 3, I want you to start wiggling your fingers and your toes. I want you to start saying goodbye to your place of sanctuary but remind yourself that you can return as often as you'd like. 1 . . . 2 . . . 3 . . .*

Encourage participants to try somatic quieting and other relaxation exercises at home. Emphasize that, like physical health, good mental health and peace of mind require regular "exercise," as well as a good "diet" of activities and social contacts. Clients may want to audiotape PMR or other relaxation instructions. There are also a number of commercial relaxation CDs that might be helpful.

## Medications for Anxiety

There are a number of medications that can help decrease the symptoms of anxiety. These drugs range from relatively mild and slow acting to rapid and sedating. Some drugs can be taken on an as-needed basis, while others must be taken every day. The best drug for a particular patient depends on the kind of symptoms he is having. Give examples of common drugs and discuss their use with the client.

## Drugs Taken Every Day

Most medications in this class are antidepressants. Although they were initially developed for depression, they also have a beneficial effect on anxiety. Typically, these medications are only used for anxiety when a client meets DSM-IV-TR criteria for an anxiety disorder such as generalized anxiety, panic disorder, social anxiety disorder, etc. They are not useful for occasional flare-ups of anxiety symptoms. For further information on adherence, typical amount of time until therapeutic effects, etc. refer back to the medication section of Session 4.

### Examples of Drugs Taken Every Day for Anxiety Disorders

- Paroxetine (Paxil®)

- Sertraline (Zoloft®)

- Venlafaxine (Effexor®)

- Buspirone (BuSpar®)

## Drugs Taken As Needed

Most medications in this category are "sedative-hypnotics," particularly in the class of drugs called benzodiazepines. These drugs are very effective at stopping or preventing anxiety symptoms. These drugs vary widely in their time to onset and the duration of effects. Longer acting medications like clonazepam should be used for longer lasting symptom relief, while shorter acting drugs like lorazepam can be used for more immediate but shorter effects. Most of these drugs have side effects that include drowsiness, lethargy, dizziness, poor concentration, and an increased risk of falls. Many of these drugs also carry the risk of physical dependence, although most patients who take them do so safely and responsibly.

### Examples of Drugs Taken for Short Periods of Time or as Needed

- Lorazepam (Ativan®)

- Alprazolam (Xanax®)

- Clonazepam (Klonopin®)

- Diazepam (Valium®)

If participants are interested in trying medications for anxiety, they should ask their health care providers for more information. Since most clients will already be on multiple medications, they should be sure to ask about drug–drug interactions and impact on liver function.

Individual and group therapy can also help decrease the symptoms of anxiety. Explain that therapy often helps identify the cause of the anxiety and helps generate solutions on how to solve it. It can also be helpful just to share one's fears with another person and get some advice or support. Therapy can be helpful for clients with full-blown anxiety disorders, as well as for clients who may only have residual anxiety symptoms.

Explain that a number of different types of therapy have proven helpful, but cognitive-behavioral therapy (CBT) has once again been shown to be the most effective. Although there are many variants of CBT for anxiety, most include training in how to breathe, how to relax major muscle groups, and how to think about problems in ways that are helpful, and some element of being exposed to and coping with the feared object or situation. Like CBT for depression, CBT for anxiety teaches clients practical coping skills that they can integrate into everyday life. Treatment is usually short term (5–10 visits), but it can be as long or as short as needed.

Given the possible high prevalence of trauma in this client population, it may be helpful to specifically mention CBT-like therapy options for PTSD. Leading therapies include exposure with cognitive restructuring and reprocessing and stress inoculation training. Current PTSD studies are testing the effectiveness of combining medications with psychotherapy. If clients are interested in other types of counseling in addition to this program, their health care providers can help with a referral for treatment.

## Review of Steps for Dealing with Anxiety

Review the three steps in coping with anxiety:

Step 1: Identify the cause(s) of anxiety.

Step 2: Choose an intervention that addresses the root problem and/or the symptoms (e.g., self-help, meds, and therapy).

Step 3: Adopt new mental health habits to minimize future anxiety.

Ask clients to consider which anxiety management strategies they would like to include in their ongoing mental hygiene program (see homework exercise in workbook). Clients may first want to test out several different strategies before settling on a regular practice. Emphasize that mental health (just like physical health) requires regular maintenance and attention.

## Homework

✎ Have client complete the My Symptoms of Anxiety form.

✎ Have client make a plan for treating his anxiety, if relevant.

✎ Have client start filling out My Mental Hygiene Program form.

✎ Have client practice at least one mental hygiene intervention such as diaphragmatic breathing, PMR, or guided imagery on a daily basis or as often as he is able.

✎ Encourage client to continue practicing one prior skill—e.g., A-B-C-D exercise, problem solving, or pleasant activity scheduling.

## FAQs from Clients

1. I know I'm anxious but I also know I'm sick—very sick. How can I tell if my shortness of breath (or other symptom) is anxiety or my medical illness? What if it's another heart attack? Can I really afford not to go to the ER?

   *A: It can be very difficult to distinguish between symptoms of anxiety and symptoms of other medical diseases. It is best to take a conservative approach and first seek out the highest level of care (e.g., if you have chest pains, go to the ER). However, after you have had a complete physical workup, discuss the symptoms with your physician. She may have some pointers on what sorts of symptoms require an emergency visit and which are probably due to anxiety. Regardless, you should adopt new mental health habits that will reduce any possible anxiety symptoms. Treating anxiety and treating your disease can happen at the same time.*

2. All this stuff about anxiety sounds just like the material about stress. What's the difference between stress and anxiety?

    *A: Anxiety and stress are very closely related. It might be easiest to think of stress as a particular kind of anxiety. Remember that anxiety is triggered by the perception of a threat and doubts about your ability to cope (very similar to primary and secondary appraisals). However, the term anxiety also includes a number of anxiety disorders such as panic disorder, generalized anxiety disorder, or social anxiety disorder. While these disorders have a stress component, they are much more than a stress reaction. If you don't have an anxiety disorder, it is probably okay to use anxiety and stress interchangeably.*

3. My life is too crowded and too busy to find the quiet time for these relaxation exercises. How am I supposed to do them if I am never alone or if my house is never quiet?

    *A: The demands of everyday life often pull us away from the things we need to do to stay healthy. It is hard to find time to relax, just as it is hard to find time to exercise or eat right. However, your health—including your mental health—needs to be a priority. You deserve the time and the investment. If your home is too chaotic, try to find another place to practice relaxation such as a library, church, doctor's waiting room, or other quiet hideaway. You may even consider taking extra time in the bathroom to relax. Remember that some of the strategies like deep breathing can be done anywhere under any circumstances.*

4. My doctor tells me that there's a good chance I might die in the next few years. This really scares me! How is some breathing exercise supposed to help with that?

    *A: I'm sorry you've gotten such news. It can be very scary to think about death, dying, or our eventual decline. The relaxation exercises aren't intended to make a fear like that go away. They are intended to help you feel more stable, more centered, and more able to face the things you cannot change. Remember that the other steps in anxiety management ask you to reflect, problem solve, seek support, or do whatever needs to be done to face the pressing problem. Relaxation is just one option on a large menu. Turn to Session 11 in this program to find skills that might help you cope with what we all must face eventually.*

# Session 6 | *Illness and Mood: Anger*

*(Corresponds to session 6 of the workbook)*

## Materials Needed

- Flip chart or board
- My Anger Habits Worksheet
- Anger Solutions Worksheet
- Acceptance and Forgiveness Worksheet

## Outline

- Set agenda
- Review homework
- Define anger and discuss common expressions of anger
- Discuss how to identify angry feelings
- Discuss how to identify the source of anger
- Discuss how to problem solve around anger
- Discuss how to ease one's mind
- Discuss acceptance and forgiveness
- Assign homework

## Setting the Agenda

Set the agenda by referring to the session outline. Ask the client if any other topics should be added. If an agenda becomes too long, collaboratively prioritize the items. Add additional practice of earlier skills if needed.

## Homework Review

Review the homework from the last session (symptoms of anxiety, anxiety treatment plan, somatic quieting, and mental hygiene plan). If clients meet diagnostic criteria for an anxiety disorder, advocate treatment. Identify any obstacles to completing homework and problem solve as needed. Remind the client that homework is key to getting the most out of the program.

Many of the skills taught in the last and earlier sessions may need to be carried forward into this session—e.g., somatic quieting, self-monitoring, problem solving, A-B-C-D exercise, etc. If clients do not feel comfortable with these basic skills, they may benefit from additional practice and training.

## Definition of Anger

You may want to start the discussion on anger with the following dialogue:

> *Being sick isn't easy. Being sick isn't fair. You don't deserve to suffer and you don't deserve all of these difficult changes in your life. So why did it happen? Why you? Why like this? Why now? These and similar questions are common for people coping with medical illnesses. We've learned to appreciate justice and fairness. We've learned to be responsible and accept the consequences of our actions. But sometimes the scales just don't seem to even out. Sometimes things just don't feel right or just. Understandably, you might be left feeling angry or robbed.*

Review the following common expressions of anger. Ask the client if any of these sound familiar.

- *You snap at your family or friends over little things.*

- *You withdraw from normal social contacts.*

- *You see happy, healthy people and resent them.*

- *You feel like you're losing or questioning your religious faith.*

- *You feel a hard, burning knot of anger twisting in your stomach.*

- *You have tension headaches, neck aches, or backaches.*

- *Your mind keeps going around and around with thoughts about the injustice of your situation.*

- *You have trouble sleeping or relaxing.*

- *You drink more alcohol or take medications to make you feel numb or forget.*

- *You feel entitled to special treatment and consideration.*

- *You feel anger or blame toward the medical profession.*

- *You skip your medications or ignore your doctor's recommendations out of spite.*

- *Your attitude toward life becomes bitter and pessimistic.*

- *You feel a need to blame and accuse others for your misfortune.*

Be sure to normalize participants' feelings of anger regardless of the cause or target. Emphasize that everyone gets angry sometimes. It's a normal and natural emotion just like any other. Depression is about the perception of loss. Anxiety is the perception of threat coupled with doubts about the ability to cope. In contrast, anger is usually triggered by a perceived injustice or violation of what is thought to be rightfully ours. It is a natural response to perceived unfairness or mistreatment. Anger motivates us to acknowledge the injustice and do something to correct it, protect ourselves, and protect our loved ones. Unlike depression, anger makes people feel powerful, righteous, and energized to action. Like anxiety, anger uses a lot of energy and should be used only when it is constructive—i.e., when there has been a real injustice that can be changed or corrected.

Given anger's ability to "highjack" our physiology, thoughts, and behaviors, it comes as no surprise that being chronically angry or hostile can have notable effects on our health. Hostility or cynicism has long been considered one of the primary personality factors associated with negative health outcomes. Although the research is sometimes contradictory, high hostility (especially in men under 60) has been related to heart attacks, cardiovascular disease, and overall earlier deaths (Iribarren et al., 2000, 2005; Surtees et al., 2005). Even if a client's anger isn't chronic or intense enough to have long-term health effects, it can certainly be responsible for much interpersonal conflict, sleepless nights, and unnecessary suffering.

When anger arises, we really have three options—expression, suppression, or defusing. We can verbally or physically express our anger in a variety of ways that are constructive or destructive. We can suppress our anger or push it onto a back burner and hope it doesn't come out as sulking or in other indirect or passive–aggressive ways. Or finally, we can defuse our anger by soothing our tense minds and bodies and addressing the situation that triggered the anger. Explain that just like with habits of mind, we have habits in how we experience and respond to anger. Some clients have lifelong habits of intensely expressing anger while others may have learned that anger is "bad" and should always be suppressed.

With life-altering events such as serious medical illness, it's sometimes easy to get stuck with a lot of anger that has nowhere to go. There's often no clear person or thing that can be blamed. There is no clear injustice or violation of rights. Even if an injustice can be identified, it is hard to correct or find retribution. In short, a serious medical illness may challenge some of the basic assumptions we have about the fairness of life or the basic rights to which we think we are entitled. We may be left feeling shocked, confused, afraid, depressed, or very angry. This session hopes to assist clients in detecting their anger early and mindfully choosing how they would like to respond.

Although there is no foolproof way to cope with anger, the following steps might offer some assistance. Remind clients that these steps closely match those followed when coping with anxiety—identifying the feeling, uncovering the cause, and problem solving. Depending on the situation, the most helpful strategy could be constructive expression, temporary suppression, defusion, or some combination of these three.

## Step 1: Identify Your Feelings

Remind the client that sometimes feelings can lurk outside of awareness. We can be upset and not realize it. Clients have already practiced how to self-monitor thoughts and activities. They should also learn how to monitor bodily sensations and identify when these sensations provide information about their current emotional state. Ask clients what physical clues alert them to the fact that they are angry. How does the anger feel? Where does it reside? Are there additional behavioral or cognitive clues that tell them they are angry? Other clues include having friends or family mention that they seem angry, having any of the "symptoms" of anger discussed in the previous section, or having angry daydreams or fantasies. Ask clients to turn to the My Anger Habits Worksheet in the workbook. As with depression and anxiety, clients are asked to list ways in which anger tends to manifest for them. Clients should also start reflecting on their habits of anger—i.e., if they tend to express, suppress, or defuse it. These anger habits may help explain why their anger tends to escalate, simmer, or fade away. Clients will later evaluate how well their current habits work and may try other ways of responding to anger.

### Questions Clients Can Ask Themselves

- Am I angry? What signs or symptoms do I have?

- How angry am I?

- How can others tell when I am angry? How does anger come out?

- Do I allow myself to feel angry? If yes, how do I express anger?

- If no, how do I suppress anger? What happens if I suppress it? Does it come out in other ways?

- Do I tend to defuse anger? How? Does it work?

- Where do my habits of anger come from? Any family similarities?

Remind clients that anger is usually about the perception of injustice perpetrated by another person, place, event, or thing. However, anger is not necessarily rational; feelings don't always make perfect sense. Feelings are sources of information on how we're doing or what's going on in the world, but they are also very much influenced by personal history, physical well-being, and other factors. Many people who are physically ill are angry at some point but they can't really blame it on anyone or anything. Some people get mad at God. Some people blame themselves or their past health habits (e.g., smoking). Some people feel like they are being punished. Others blame genetics or even environmental pollution. Sometimes anger is simply an expression of suffering. It can be an "idiom of distress" or a way of letting others know we are in pain, we are afraid, or we are depressed. Some researchers have argued that anger is one of the few socially acceptable ways for men in particular to express vulnerability and pain (Eisler et al., 1988).

Before initiating the steps of problem solving (Step 3 below), it is important to determine if the "problem" lies within or outside of the client—i.e., is the anger about the client's inner pain or about an external grievance (or perhaps a bit of both). This process of identification is similar to identifying the stressor, as discussed in Session 3. Once identified, the client can move on to problem-focused (see Step 3) or emotion-focused (see Step 4) coping. At this identification stage, it is important to suspend judgment. The client is not assessing the rationality or constructiveness of being angry at that particular time—just where the anger is coming from. When anger is detected, the client uses self-inquiry to understand the cause.

### Questions Clients Can Ask Themselves

- What made me angry? Was it a person, place, thing, event, or idea?

- What happened right before I felt angry? What was going through my mind?

- Who am I angry with? Does the person know I am angry?

- What's the injustice? What "right" has been violated?

■ Is this anger really about me feeling sad? Grieving? Being in physical pain? Being sick? Is this anger my way of expressing distress?

Discuss any ideas clients have about the source(s) of their anger. When exploring the cause of anger, it is important to remember that anger has inertia. Once set in motion, it is easier to become angry about any number of things that are unrelated to the original cause. When clients are angry in the moment, they should remember to "rewind the tape" to uncover what initially set off that episode of anger. Uncovering the accurate cause of anger will be important to finding a resolution. Remembering that anger has inertia will be important when moving on to other activities after an angry episode.

## Step 3: Problem Solve

After identifying the feeling and its source, the next step is to decide what, if anything, can be done about it. Not all problems can or should be "fixed." Is the problem changeable? Is the cause of the anger someone or something that is amenable to intervention? Is the cause something in the present or something in the past that can no longer be accessed? If the problem or cause of the anger is deemed changeable, remind the client to apply the steps of problems solving—i.e., clearly identify the problem, list potential solutions, then choose a solution based on the pros and cons of each option. It can be helpful to identify the problem category using the following questions:

1. Is it a problem involving another person? (See Session 8 on communication and conflict negotiation)
   a. Is it something the person did wrong? Can she make atonement or compensation? How can the scales be balanced? Would an apology help?
   b. How much of the anger is about a recent event, and how much is from the buildup of your past with this person?
   c. What is the other person's perspective?

2. Does it seem tied to the management of the disease?
   a. Would improved communication with your medical team help? Have you rallied all the professional support available to you? (See Session 8)

b. Is it about new symptoms or a symptom that as gotten worse? (See Session 9 on symptom management)

c. Is the fear based primarily in fear and uncertainty about your illness? (See Session 5 on anxiety management)

3. Is the source of the anger mostly coming from inside? (See Step 4 below)

a. Is your anger mostly about your way of thinking? (See Session 2 on types of thinking and habits of mind)

b. Are you angry because you are depressed, lonely, or feeling hopeless? (See Session 4 on depression)

c. Have you lost touch with your faith or source of spiritual strength? (See Session 11)

4. Is the anger reasonable and expected?

a. Are you just really cranky and irritable right now?

b. Are you taking this too personally?

c. Is your thinking balanced, fair, and nonjudgmental?

d. What would an outside observer say about this situation?

If the cause of the anger is deemed changeable, the client should begin to develop a plan on how to respond. If the current level of arousal is too high, the client might first want to practice some defusing (see Step 4) then address the situation. At the end of the session, you will help the client start an Anger Solution Worksheet using a recent example from the client's life.

## Step 4: Ease Your Mind

Explain that sometimes the source of our anger cannot be directly addressed or corrected. Sometimes the anger comes from inside or it comes from wounds received long, long ago. If the client is mad at the universe or someone who's passed away, there's really nothing practical that can be done to change the situation. However, clients can do something to change the way they feel. They can defuse the angry feelings rather than trying to solve a problem that has no solution (i.e., they can use more emotion-focused coping and mood management strategies). It may be important to address the myth that "letting it out" (e.g., screaming or hitting something) helps release and diminish angry feelings. Recent research has shown that aggressive behavior (meant to serve as a sort of release or catharsis) actually amplifies anger and aggression (Anderson & Bushman, 2002). Although unclear at this point, "letting it out" may not work because people tend to ruminate while they are being aggressive. On the other hand, physical exercise without rumination about the perceived violation may still be beneficial.

Here are a few ideas to help clients defuse anger.

## Challenge Habits of Mind

As learned in Sessions 2 and 3, everyone takes thinking shortcuts. Everyone develops habits of mind that sometimes serve us well but sometimes create unnecessary pain and suffering. Remind clients of the thought exercises they have learned—the A-B-C-D exercise and balanced, flexible, nonjudgmental thinking. In the case of anger, thinking is often judgmental (a person, place, or thing is labeled and judged), thinking is inflexible, and only one unbalanced side is considered. Cognitive moderation of anger does not imply that anger is not justified. It simply lowers the level of physical and emotional arousal so we can think and act more clearly if and when the need arises. Staying angry usually hurts us the most.

## Distraction

Anger has inertia: once started, it is difficult to stop. Anger affects our bodies but it also hijacks our thoughts, causing us to ruminate obsessively about the perceived injury. Sometimes this rumination only worsens the situation or deepens our anger. When one's mind feels stuck this way, it helps to take it elsewhere by using distraction. Suggest that clients try reading a book, watching a movie, inviting someone over for a visit, or doing an art or writing project. Whatever distraction is chosen, it needs to be absorbing. Have clients come up with a few potent distractors that are realistic and effective given their individual situations.

## Relaxation

Review and practice the breathing, PMR, and guided imagery exercises from Session 5. Remind participants that anger creates tension, but relaxation washes tension and anger away. It is impossible to remain consumed by anger when physically relaxed. Relaxation activities may work in two ways: they induce a relaxation response but they also serve as a distractor that prevents further rumination and elaboration of the perceived violation.

## Focus on the Positive

Although there are losses and injustices in everyone's life, there are also triumphs and reasons to be grateful. Humans are probably hard-wired to notice and remember the negative aspects first. Noticing threats, losses, and violations probably conferred a survival advantage at one time. A low, depressed, or irritable mood can further deepen selective attention to negative events (Fredrickson, 2001). A new and rapidly growing area of psychology called "positive psychology" is helping us to understand this bias and to place greater value on successes, triumphs, and meaningful relationships (Snyder & Lopez, 2005). It is important to learn how to "push back" when a negative kind of focus is not constructive. It is important to make a conscious effort to reestablish balance. Establishing balance means actively and consciously recognizing the positive aspects and taking a moment to savor them (i.e., a sort of positive rumination). In Sessions 10 and 11, participants may choose to start a gratitude journal or other exercises that encourage a positive focus. They might also want to create a list of "wins," life successes, pleasurable memories, etc.

## Help Others

Sometimes we can make meaning out of pain and sadness by using our experience and wisdom to help others. Encourage participants to think about volunteering, calling a friend who needs them, or writing about their experiences in an inspirational way. Everyone has stories to share that might be helpful. What does the client have to offer?

## Improve Your Health

Sometimes physical exercise and improving one's diet can help a person feel better both mentally and physically. Encourage participants to try eating healthier foods that make them feel better (e.g., more complex carbohydrates, less processed and sugary foods). They may also try releasing their anger through moderate physical exercise (they should speak with their doctors before starting any exercise program). It is important to remember that clients should not ruminate about things that make them angry when they are exercising. Exercise physiologists suggest that exercise works in several ways. First, exercise affects stress hormones, or the chemicals that make us feel tense, uptight, or angry. Secondly, exercise causes a release of endogenous opiates or our body's natural, soothing painkillers that increase a feeling of well-being. Third, exercise improves overall fitness and flexibility, which may decrease pain, increase endurance, and gradually promote a healthier mind and body (Robergs & Roberts, 1997). For clients with physical disabilities or chronic pain, physical therapy may be a therapeutic and safe outlet.

## Medication

Certain medications can help alleviate the negative effects of stress, anxiety, depression, and anger. If applicable, clients should speak with their doctors about whether this option fits for them. See Sessions 4 and 5 on depression and anxiety for a discussion of common medication options. Other less common medications might include mood stabilizers or drugs used for high blood pressure that generally dampen arousal (e.g., beta-blockers such as Atenolol).

## Get Support

Sometimes just telling another person about one's anger can be helpful. Encourage clients to let others know how they feel and that they only want them to listen. It is important, however, that talking about it not become elaboration and escalation of anger. Instruct clients to share the "strong" feelings of anger but also to be sure to share the more vulnerable feelings that lie underneath. It is difficult for listeners to connect with anger and offer useful support. Anger repels; it is much easier to empathize with what might lie underneath (see Session 7 on getting support).

For clients especially interested in anger management, you may want to recommend the following books (see Appendix for more information):

*Anger Kills: Seventeen Strategies for Controlling the Hostility that Can Harm Your Health* by R. Williams and V. Williams

*When Anger Hurts: Quieting the Storm Within* by M. McKay, P. Rogers, and J. McKay

## Step 5: Accept and Forgive

Sometimes the most constructive way to cope is to simply let go and move on. Explain that accepting a situation or forgiving an injustice doesn't mean surrender, resignation, or giving up. It doesn't mean forgetting. It doesn't indicate weakness or passivity. Sometimes acceptance and forgiveness are the hardest but strongest things a person can do.

## Acceptance and Letting Go

You may want to use the following in your discussion:

> *We've all heard the famous serenity prayer: "God grant me the courage to change the things I can, the serenity to accept the things I can't, and the wisdom to know the difference." The fact is, we simply cannot control or change everything, no matter how hard we try. You cannot make your illness go away. You cannot roll back time and erase past mistakes. You can only accept the situation as it is and move onward with your life. You can't change the problem but you CAN change the way you feel. Sometimes people feel better when they accept that there is nothing they can do to get better.*

You may conceptualize acceptance as "letting go" or giving up active efforts to change what may be an unchangeable situation. Although the unchangeable situation may cause suffering, it is the repeated (and failed) efforts to change it that also cause frustration and suffering. Discuss how sometimes letting go is the only solution. Review the phrases in the workbook that can help in the process of letting go.

## Forgiveness

Explain that forgiving someone or something for a wrong that occurred doesn't need to have moral or religious connotations. It really only involves ourselves and the anger we choose to hold or release. Forgiveness does not mean legal pardon, making excuses, or reconciliation. It simply means choosing to let go of past injuries so we can invest our limited energy elsewhere. The forgiver receives the most benefit. The forgiver might also be forgiving himself for past mistakes. Either way, forgiveness is an ongoing process that starts with making a choice—the choice to release anger and move on. It is important to remember that the process of forgiveness can be a slow, developmental effort that involves many steps, as follows (Flanigan, 1994).

*Step 1:* Identify the insult, injury, or violation that has occurred. This includes striving for balanced thinking and owning your own role in the situation.

*Step 2:* Own the outcome. This involves admitting that the illness or injury is permanent and is now yours to cope with. Although the external wound might have healed, if you are still angry or changed in some way, the injury continues. Own it. It is now part of who you are.

*Step 3:* Determine accountability. Someone or something is held accountable for causing the harm. You might find that you are accountable or that no one can be held accountable.

*Step 4:* Balance the scales. You are not a hopeless and helpless victim. Do something to rectify the problem if possible (see Step 3 of this session or Session 8 on conflict resolution).

*Step 5:* Choose to forgive or release a grudge. Try empathizing with the responsible party. What was she thinking or feeling? What was it like for her growing up? How was or is she hurting? How much is staying angry costing you? Costing her? This step is not about making excuses. It is about finding explanations that help us better understand why something happened. It may decrease overpersonalization and soothe hurt feelings.

Have the client turn to the Acceptance and Forgiveness Worksheet in the workbook. At this point, the client is expected to identify interpersonal conflicts or other areas in need of work. Later sessions will explore conflict resolution. For more information on the process of forgiveness, recommend books such as the following (see the Appendix for more information):

*Forgiving the Unforgivable: Overcoming the Bitter Legacy of Intimate Wounds* by Beverly Flanigan

*Forgive for Good: A Proven Prescription for Health and Happiness* by Fred Luskin

## Importance of Reconciliation at the End of Life

Many believe that acceptance and forgiveness are especially important at the end of life (Byock, 1997). Although much of life may have been about work, finances, or daily stressors, in the end it is our relationships that matter the most. If there are ongoing conflicts or unresolved differences, it may be important to work for a reconciliation while there is still time. The "advantage" of having a chronic illness (in contrast to a sudden and unexpected death) is that it gives one time to do the "work" of closing out one's life. That may include forgiving oneself, forgiving others, and expressing love and gratitude.

Remind clients that managing anger and irritability is an ongoing process and they don't have to go it alone. Help them begin the Anger Solutions Worksheet to practice the five steps of anger management presented in this session. As preparation for the next session, they should try to identify what works for them and where they get stuck.

✎ Have client complete the My Anger Habits Worksheet.

✎ Have client practice the five steps of anger management using the Anger Solutions Worksheet.

✎ Have client identify and begin reflection using the Acceptance and Forgiveness Worksheet.

✎ Have client continue relaxation or other skill practice as needed.

## FAQs from Clients

1. These anger exercises are slow but my anger is very quick. How can I stop that angry impulse from occurring in the first place instead of always having to go back and fix what I messed up?

   *A: A very good point. Angry impulses can be lightning fast since they come from a very primitive part of our brain. Our slower, "thinking" brain just can't compete in terms of initial speed. However, you don't have to react to an initial angry impulse. Just notice it, then immediately breathe, release, and begin talking yourself down. You'll get pretty good at this with practice. Exercise, stress management, medications, and improving your social supports can sometimes help you have a "longer fuse." However, some people just have a lower threshold for anger no matter what they do. They need to practice how to capture and reduce those angry urges.*

2. Isn't it good to be angry sometimes? Don't you need to stand up for yourself or fight injustices?

   *A: Absolutely. This session is meant to help you decide when your anger is just and useful versus those times when your anger isn't that helpful. Remember, though, that even "good" anger requires energy. If you are short on energy, be sure to pick your battles wisely.*

3.  Are there any risks to always suppressing anger? Does anger suppression harm your health? Does it increase your risk of "exploding" and doing a lot of damage?

    *A: A lot of current anger research looks at "anger-out" versus "anger-in" styles of expression. "Anger-out" is outwardly directing anger or hostility to other people or things. "Anger-in" is suppressing anger or turning anger inward on yourself. Some studies show that anger suppression (fuming but keeping it inside) does negatively affect cardiovascular function, but it may vary by gender, age, and other variables. At this point, your best bet to maximize your health is to reduce your overall anger so there is nothing to direct either inwardly or outwardly.*

4.  My parents (or spouse or others) were abusive and hurtful and mean. They are out of my life now but I still hold onto this intense rage that comes up whenever I think about what I went through. I know that holding onto my rage only hurts me, but I can't seem to let it go. What can I do?

    *A: Remember that forgiveness starts with a choice. You choose to begin the process of letting go of a past injury. You make that choice for yourself and not for the person who hurt you. Remember that forgiveness can be a slow, developmental process that takes work and persistence. Don't be discouraged if it doesn't come right away. You've probably gone over what happened a thousand times, so stop replaying that tape. Start thinking about why you want to let it go. Start to explore the social, environmental, or other original circumstances around the injury that might help you understand why it happened (it doesn't excuse it but it may explain it). Turn to the steps for forgiveness in Session 6. Can you develop empathy for the flawed person who hurt you? Can you develop empathy for yourself? It often helps to seek out additional counseling to get past these powerful injuries. You need a place to process and a place to grow.*

# Module 3
## Social Supports

# Session 7 *Social Support Network*

*(Corresponds to session 7 of the workbook)*

## Materials Needed

- Flip chart or board
- My Social Support Network Diagram
- My Thoughts about Social Supports Worksheet

## Outline

- Set agenda
- Review homework
- Define and review types of support
- Help client identify social support network
- Help client evaluate social supports
- Discuss the steps for expressing support needs
- Assign homework

## Setting the Agenda

Set the agenda by referring to the session outline. Ask the client if any other topics should be added. If an agenda becomes too long, collaboratively prioritize the items. Be sure to periodically include feedback from the last session as an agenda item to check in with client satisfaction and possible evolving needs.

## Homework Review

Review the homework from the last session (e.g., signs of anger, steps in dealing with anger, acceptance and forgiveness, relaxation or other "defusing" strategies). Identify any obstacles to completing homework and problem solve as needed. At this point, the client should have a good grasp of stress basics, relaxation, effective coping, and mood management for depression, anxiety, and anger. Depending on the client's needs, more time might need to be spent on earlier sessions. This might mean added sessions or simply extra homework assignments in the specified area. Clients may ask for more time to talk about acceptance and forgiveness. Review the steps of forgiveness if necessary, but remind the client that it will be an ongoing, sometimes slow process.

## Definition and Types of Social Support

Engage the client in a dialogue about social support. How does the client define this term? Why is it important? Tell the client that what we mean by "social support network" is simply the people in our lives who are there for us when we need them. Support can be emotional, informational, or practical. It can be long distance or in person. It can be ongoing or one time only. Social support is something we all need, especially when we're ill. (Although pets can be wonderful "social" support, this session focuses on support from other people. For especially isolated or socially anxious clients, pet support may be a starting point.) Review the following types of support and elicit examples from the client.

## Types of Support

*Emotional:* Behaviors and words that make you feel cared for, understood, and supported—for example, a kind word, crying together, or holding hands. Some would classify "spiritual support" in this category (e.g., praying, meditating together).

*Informational:* Includes advice, information, or suggestions on how to deal with a particular situation. The coping exercises in Session 3 (where the stressor was broken down into manageable pieces and the steps of problem solving were applied) were a form of informational support.

*Practical:* Support can be practical actions such as driving you to an appointment or doing your laundry. It can also be providing practical objects or resources such as money.

## Giving and Getting Support

Discuss how we all give and receive varying kinds of support throughout our lives. Sometimes being ill means we need a lot of each kind of support. Sometimes being ill means we lose friends and supports, or have a lot of conflicts and misunderstandings with loved ones. Those conflicts often arise from differences between the kind of support that is needed or expected and the kind of support that is actually received. For example, a client may return from a doctor's appointment really needing to vent and get emotional support. Instead, the client's significant other starts giving advice and problem solving (i.e., giving informational support instead of emotional support). The client feels unheard and unsupported while the significant other wonders what went wrong. Both people are at fault in this scenario. The client should have expressed her needs more clearly and the significant other should have asked instead of just jumping in with advice.

Another common problem has been called "compassion fatigue" or caregiver burnout. If the tasks of caregiving are chronic and overwhelming, caregivers sometimes grow impatient or resentful. The caregivers then end up feeling guilty about their negative feelings, causing them to be even more stressed. They truly want to help and meet all of the client's needs, but they are only human and can only do so much. Just as clients need to be aware of and express their needs, caregivers also need to be attuned to what they need as caregivers. Often this might mean a few days off, respite care, or creating a care schedule in which others take "shifts" to help the client. Other ideas on caring for caregivers are provided near the end of this session.

Ask clients to think about the people in their social support network. Have them complete the My Social Support Network Diagram in the workbook. This diagram provides a place to record the people who support the client and how close they are to her. Ask clients to identify what kinds of support these people are best at delivering (i.e., emotional, informational, or practical). Explain that if we have an idea of each individual's strengths, we'll know who is most likely to give us what we need.

This exercise can provide important information to guide the rest of this session. If the client's diagram contains no or few supports, a significant portion of session time should be devoted to ways to increase the number of social supports. Clients should be encouraged to include medical professionals, neighbors, pets, or others as potential supports, even if they are listed in the outer circles of the diagram. Research suggests only one close relationship is needed for health protective effects, but several individuals might be needed if care demands are high (Mookadam & Arthur, 2004). If the client's diagram has a sufficient number of individuals but no supports are near the inner circle of the diagram, part of the session should be devoted to ways to increase intimacy in a relationship (i.e., strengthen emotional bonds). The next section on evaluating social supports can assist clients in making decisions about the number and closeness of supports they personally need. If both the quantity and quality of supports seem sufficient, most of the discussion can be spent on how to express needs and elicit helpful responses. Given the stress of caregiving, nearly all clients should consider ways to care for their social support network.

## Evaluating Social Supports

Refer to the completed My Social Support Network Diagram. Help clients evaluate their social support network (i.e., are there enough people? are they close enough? do they get the job done?) by asking the following questions:

- *How are your current supports doing in terms of meeting your needs?*

- *What grade would you give the overall social support you currently receive?*

- *What do you think is missing?*

- *What support are you grateful for?*

- *Do you need to add new people to your list?*

- *Do you wish your social supports were closer to you? Who do you want to be in your inner circle?*

If current support is not satisfactory, help the client determine which of the three most common causes are to blame:

1. Lack of intimacy or closeness to current supports

2. New (more) people need to be added to the support network.

3. Although number and closeness of supports is okay, the client needs to improve his skills in identifying his needs and asking for support.

Assist clients in brainstorming on how to expand their list of supporters and increase intimacy to best meet their needs. Remind them that support can come in all shapes and sizes. Some sources of support that we sometimes don't think about include religion or spirituality, neighbors, nature and the outdoors, on-line chat rooms and groups, etc. (see the workbook for more examples).

## Expressing Support Needs

Emphasize to the client that when we are experiencing stress, it is essential that we be able to express ourselves to get the support we need. We might need to vent. We might need a hug. We might need financial support. We might need to let someone know about physical pain or trouble breathing. Tell the client that it is important to do the following:

1. Realize you need help and what specific kind of help you need.

2. Believe that you deserve help.

3. Believe that expressing your need and getting help will be useful.

4. Assertively ask the person best suited to your needs to help you.

5. Accept help graciously.

6. Nurture and care for your social supports.

Work through all the steps with the client as follows.

## Step 1: Realize You Need Help and What Specific Kind of Help You Need

Use an example such as the following. If the client has already shared a personally relevant example in an earlier session, adapt accordingly.

> *A client is in physical pain despite taking his pain medication as prescribed. He hates to complain and he knows his spouse doesn't like to see him hurting, but this pain is almost unbearable. He needs help. But what kind and from whom? He might need all three kinds of support from more than one person.*
>
> Emotional: *His spouse can offer comfort and empathy.*
>
> Informational: *His doctor or nurse could provide more information on pain medication or ways to manage pain.*
>
> Practical: *His caregiver could give him more medications, a massage, a hot compress, or drive him to the emergency room.*

## Step 2: Believe that You Deserve Help

Initiate a dialogue with the client similar to the following:

> *Sometimes being seriously ill means feeling guilty and feeling like a burden. It seems like you are draining your loved ones. It may seem like you deserve your illness or brought it on yourself. Or it might just feel like you don't have a right to ask for help. But nobody deserves to suffer alone. There is nothing noble about excluding your family and friends from your life—even if your life seems mostly full of sickness and need at the moment. You should do all you can do for yourself, but no one can do it all alone. Now is your time to receive. You deserve as much compassion as you would extend to others. Be compassionate to yourself and allow others to help you. You deserve it. Give others a chance to show their love by accepting their support.*

At this point, have clients turn to the workbook exercise My Thoughts about Social Supports. Ask them to write down any thoughts they have about whether they deserve support and if they believe they will get it. If needed, clients can use A-B-C-D or thought-balancing skills to rewrite these thoughts into more helpful forms. You may wait to have the client rewrite the thoughts until the end of the session.

## Step 3: Believe that Expressing Your Need and Getting Help Will Be Useful

Initiate a dialogue with the client similar to the following:

> *This step is all about hope—not hope for a cure, but hope that asking for and getting help will make a difference in how you feel. When you are sick or in pain it's hard not to feel hopeless. It seems like you've tried everything. It seems like asking for help just won't do any good. No one will respond. Why bother? It's OK to be skeptical, but I encourage you to go back to square one and try again. Only this time, follow each step carefully and see if you can't improve your chances of getting the help you need. In fact, if you carefully choose whom to ask, when to ask, how to ask, and what to ask for, your chances of getting a response will be much higher. It might not work every time, but it's sure worth a try. If someone lets you down, go to someone else.*

## Step 4: Assertively Ask the Person Best Suited to Your Needs to Help You

Initiate a dialogue with the client similar to the following:

> *This step involves knowing your social supports and their strong points. It also requires knowing how to communicate effectively. Recall your social support diagram. Who was on it? What were their special strengths? After you know what kind of support you need, who on your list can provide it? Once you've picked whom you are going to ask, how do you ask? If possible, be sure to pick a time when your support person is able to consider your request and respond. Remember Step 2—you deserve support!*

## Step 5: Accept Help Graciously

Tell the client that accepting help often makes others feel useful and good about themselves. Remind the client that he would most likely do the same for others if he were able. You may want to use the following dialogue.

> *When accepting help it's important to be gracious to your helper and gracious to yourself. Sometimes accepting help can be hard to do—especially if it feels like someone is helping you all the time. You might feel like a burden. You might feel like you'll never be able to reciprocate. You might feel useless or unworthy. You might feel needy or dependent—maybe a far cry from how you used to feel before you got sick.*

> *Things have changed, and that might be very difficult to accept. Certainly no one wants to have more limitations or be able to do less. But it might be unavoidable. You can only do as much as your body and mind will allow. We change our roles several times in life—from child to teenager to young adult to young parent to middle-aged parent to grandparent to retiree. Most everyone at some point does get sick. Everyone dies at some point. It's guaranteed. Why not allow your family and loved ones to care for you? They need to be able to express their love. They may feel helpless too. They need to feel like there's something they can do. They need to repay you for all the support you've given them. Your illness might be hard for them and they might need to receive outside support for themselves, but they also need to give support—to give support to you.*

Refer clients again to the exercise My Thoughts about Social Supports. Remind clients to use their thought-balancing or A-B-C-D skills to rewrite these thoughts into more helpful forms—either now or at the end of the session.

## Step 6: Taking Care of Your Social Supports

Initiate a dialogue with the client similar to the following:

> *Being medically ill doesn't mean you can't give support to the people you care for. Who do you currently support? What types of support do*

*you give? What's your forte or strong point? Are you giving too much and feeling drained? Giving too little and not feeling useful? What can you as the person in need do to help?*

Refer patients to the workbook section How I Can Care for My Caregivers. Clients should be able to list two or three concrete (but realistic) ways in which they can care for their social supports. Have clients select strategies and schedule how and when they will put them into effect.

### Suggestions for Taking Care of Caregivers

1. Give your caregiver a vacation. Ask others to step in and take over temporarily.

2. Encourage your caregiver to get some support for himself. This may include a caregiver support group.

3. Make sure you let your caregivers know how much their care and love mean to you.

4. Involve more than one person in your care if possible. A shared load is a lighter load. Consider making a care schedule—i.e., a calendar where people can sign up for "shifts," or periods when you need support.

5. Ask your doctor, nurse, or social worker about community resources. A few key national resources are listed in the Appendix. (Since local resources will vary, the skill of knowing whom to ask and how to ask is more important.)

6. Offer your caregiver what support you're able to give—e.g., money, affection, laughter, gratitude.

7. Help your caregivers stay organized and informed—for example, invite them to doctor appointments, allow them to speak with your nurse, or provide them with medical records or vital contacts related to your health care or support.

8. Don't forget to savor the good times. Share old stories, photos, music, or things that take you back to easier times.

9. Schedule a shared pleasant activity such as music, a meal, or a movie.

Remind clients that their best bet to getting the support they need is to be aware of their needs, communicate those needs, and be willing to accept the help when and how it comes. If that doesn't work out, then together you should revisit the Social Support Network Diagram and use the problem-solving skills from Session 3 to brainstorm and test out new solutions.

## Homework

✎ Have client complete the My Social Support Network Diagram.

✎ Have client continue to evaluate his social network and identify any deficiencies.

✎ Have client complete the My Thoughts about Social Supports Worksheet.

✎ Encourage client to seek or provide new support as needed.

✎ Encourage client to continue with mood management and relaxation strategies.

## FAQs from Clients

1. I've always been taught to be independent. That's what my culture (or gender or class) values the most. How I can switch at this point and suddenly become dependent. It just doesn't work that way!

   *A: You're right. Culture, gender, and other factors greatly influence how we form relationships and how we feel about asking for and accepting care. However, no matter who you are or where you are from, you will need and give help sometime—perhaps often. You can still ask for privacy. You can still ask for things that preserve your dignity. Your accomplishments and independence of a lifetime will not be erased if you accept help and love now. Sometimes life comes full circle. Be proud of the fact that you've made it this far. Allow yourself to let loose a bit and enjoy the rewards of a life well lived.*

2. How can I make new friend if I'm sick and tired? I'll scare people away. I'm just not friendship material anymore.

   *A: You do have limitations to energy and you may have experienced changes in your physical appearance, but you are not alone. Think about a support group of others coping with an illness. Think about what you can bring to a new friendship rather than what you can't. Perhaps you can offer something another person longs for and vice versa.*

3. Everyone seems too busy with their own lives to invest the time to build intimacy. It was easy when I was young but now it's too hard. People's lives are just too full. I know it isn't personal, but it's just impossible.

   *A: People's lives can be very full and it can be very hard to find time to build intimacy. You are right not to take it personally. I encourage you to be patient and persistent. Extend several invitations, but be willing to accept "no" for an answer. If someone is unable or uninterested, move on to another person. It often takes several attempts with several people before you find someone who can and will move forward in building a closer friendship. Use other mood management strategies in the meantime so you don't get too down or discouraged.*

# Session 8  *Communication and Conflict Resolution*

*(Corresponds to session 8 of the workbook)*

## Materials Needed

- Flip chart or board
- My Ways of Communicating form
- My Communication Family Tree form
- Promoting Assertiveness form
- Shared Activities List
- My Health Care Team form

## Outline

- Set agenda
- Review homework
- Discuss the importance of good communication
- Discuss active listening
- Discuss how to express oneself effectively
- Present elements of conflict resolution
- Discuss the importance of quality time for strong relationships
- Give suggestions for getting the most out of health care
- Assign homework

## Setting the Agenda

Set the agenda by referring to the session outline. Ask the client if any other topics should be added. If an agenda becomes too long, collaboratively prioritize the items.

## Homework Review

Review the homework from the last session. You may want to reserve extra time to review the My Social Support Network Diagram. This diagram is important for diagnosing social support deficiencies and pointing to the most helpful remedies. Clients may also need assistance in rewriting their thoughts about social supports. Identify any other obstacles to completing homework and problem solve as needed. Remind the client that homework is key to getting the most out of the program.

## Importance of Good Communication

Begin with the metaphor that relationships are like cars—both need regular maintenance or they begin to have troubles and break down. We should always expect to do some minor tune-ups and sometimes a major overhaul. When one or both people in the relationship are medically ill, regular relationship maintenance is even more essential. Illness creates more support needs and may generate emotional distress or fears that get displaced onto those who are closest. "Maintenance" almost always requires clear, open communication and sharing—although the way in which that is done varies widely by cultural background. Communication and other kinds of relationship maintenance help solidify or deepen a connection and solve conflicts when they arise.

Explain that a big part of strengthening relationships involves building intimacy through good communication, sharing, caregiving, and spending time together. Though we are born with the capacity for speech and hearing, communication is an acquired skill that some say takes lifelong practice. Communication is especially hard when it involves emotionally charged issues such as illness, money, religion, and sex. To further complicate matters, each of us comes with different family and cultural traditions about how, when, and what to communicate. A relationship often involves learning to "speak the language" of your partner and vice versa.

Good communication involves work from both sides of the fence—the person speaking or communicating and the person listening. Although speaking and listening might seem natural, remind the client that good communication is a learned skill just like typing or driving a car. We need someone to show us how to do it and we have to practice. Review the following tips for good communication; the client will have a chance to practice later in the session.

## Tips for Good Communication

1. Try to assume an attitude of partnership and equality. You may not see eye to eye, but you are both valuable human beings with a perspective worth understanding.

2. Pick a good time when both of you are ready and able to talk and other demands or distractions aren't pressing.

3. Limit the discussion to the issue at hand, even though the temptation might be to do it all while you have the person there. Save other issues or conflicts for later. Don't drag in the past, since we all remember it differently.

4. After you have expressed your point of view, specify exactly what you want the other person to do.

5. Give a clear rationale about why you need the person to do this and how important it is to you.

6. Check with the other person to make sure she understood your request or the issue at hand. For example, you might say, "I just want to make sure I was able to effectively express what I need you to do. Can you tell me what you just heard?"

7. Get a clear response from the other person and double check to make sure you understood her. For example, "Good. It seems like

we're on the same page. So what is it you are able to do? . . . If I
heard you correctly, you agreed to do such-and-such. Is this right?"

8. If the other person's response is what you needed to hear, then express your gratitude or other ways it makes you feel. Then think of
   the next steps to put her response into action.

9. If the other persons' answer is not what you wanted, then try to
   understand why. Alter the request or begin negotiating an acceptable solution.

## Active Listening

Tell the client that despite common belief, listening is not a passive process. It first requires an open interest and respect for the talker and the
message. As we listen we can't help but add our own subjective interpretations and make our own connections; however, beginning with a sense
of partnership allows us to hear more of what is being said before jumping to conclusions. It takes an active effort to stay with the talker and
check to see if we've understood what they are trying to communicate.
Listening also involves giving clues that we're listening, asking questions,
and providing feedback. Review with the client the following important
points to remember.

## Tips for Listening

### Optimize Your Environment and Attitude

- Eliminate distractions such as TV, telephone, etc.

- Make sure you've eaten and/or have something to drink

- Provide privacy if necessary

- Suspend judgment and try to listen with an open mind

### Improve Your Nonverbal Cues

- Make and keep eye contact (unless cultural rules view eye contact as rude or too direct)

- Lean slightly forward toward the speaker

- Keep an open, relaxed posture

- Use nods or "uh-huhs" to indicate you're still with the speaker

### Improve Your Verbal Cues

- Use clarifying questions but don't change the subject

- Do not interrupt with your own story

- Use empathic statements ("I'm so sorry that happened") to indicate your concern

- Paraphrase what you heard after the speaker finishes to make sure you heard correctly

- Ask the speaker what she'd like you to do before jumping to action

## Obstacles to Listening

Stress that although listening might sound simple, it's not. (Ask: "How good of a listener are you? Would your significant other or friends agree? What gets in the way of you being a good listener?")

For many of us, there are common obstacles that prevent us from being good listeners. Many of them are similar to the habits of mind discussed in Session 2. These can include the following:

- Blaming, labeling, or judging

- Jumping to conclusions

- Mind reading

- Rehearsing what we want to say instead of listening

- Being distracted and thinking about something else

- Competing for status, power, or "air-time"

- Being argumentative

- Focusing on minor issues or inconsistencies

- Giving unsolicited advice

- Getting angry or irritable (usually from a perceived injustice or violation)

- Not being empathetic or able to "step in the other person's shoes"

- Being self-absorbed with our own stories

- Thinking we are "better" than the person talking

- Playing the "yes-man"

Elicit other possible obstacles from the client. Emphasize that listening is an *active* and challenging process that takes time and energy. Discuss the client's experiences with listening. Ask what she has noticed about her and others' listening patterns. Where were these patterns learned? Does the client believe these patterns are changeable?

## How to Express Oneself Effectively

As mentioned earlier, remind clients that listening is only one half of the equation. The other half involves the speaker or the person who is trying to convey her perspective or other important information. Although *speaker* implies verbal communication, it can also include written, emotional, and other nonverbal forms of discourse that convey information. There is no "right" way to communicate, but there are ways that are more or less effective in achieving the goals of the client or her family.

Have the client complete the My Ways of Communicating form in the workbook, which is divided into ways of communicating specific emotions or discussing common difficult scenarios. Remember that verbal, nonverbal, written, behavioral, and other ways of communicating should be considered. Once clients have begun capturing ways in which they tend to communicate, have them reflect on how effective these habits have been, using the following questions:

- *Do these habits work in certain contexts only? With certain people only?*

- *If they are not terribly effective or perhaps cause greater conflict, what is it that goes wrong?*

- *What is the obstacle or habit of mind that gets in the way?*

- *How much is due to you, your partner, and the situation?*

## Family Tree Exercise (optional)

If time permits, it is sometimes fruitful to have clients explore the familial and cultural roots of their communication style. Not only do these important background factors influence communication style, but they also may dictate how difficult it will be to learn new communication skills. Have clients turn to the My Communication Family Tree exercise in the workbook.

Ask the client to draw her family tree going back two generations (her immediate family, her parents and grandparents). You may want to use a simple genogram format in which a circle represents a female, a square represents a male, and a horizontal bar joining two shapes represents marriage. For example, if Rachel is a single woman with one brother and no aunts or uncles, her family tree would look like this (Fig. 8.1).

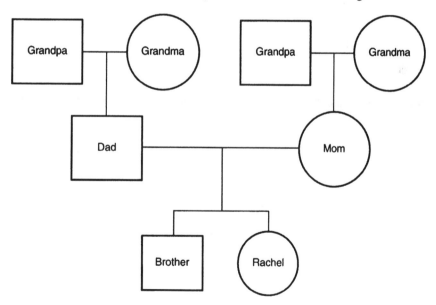

**Figure 8.1**
Example of a Family Tree

After the family tree has been drawn, ask the client to reflect on the communication style of both the immediate family and the extended family. The following prompts may guide exploration.

- *What was the overall communication style of your family? (e.g., loud and boisterous, quiet and reserved, highly emotional and expressive, stoic and serious, direct or indirect, etc.)*

- *How did people express themselves? Verbally? Written? Nonverbally?*

- *How did people listen?*

- *How well did this work? When did it cause problems?*

- *In what ways is your communication style similar to or different from your family's style?*

## Role Play Exercise (optional)

If clients need direct practice with more effective verbal communication, assist them in identifying an important conversation they need to have in the near future. Help the client identify the key message, try out a few ways to frame that message, then try it out in a role play. "Rewind" and try several different ways to communicate. You might want to intentionally role play an ineffective way to communicate for demonstration purposes (and perhaps a little humor).

## Conflict Resolution

Regardless of how strong a relationship might be, there are bound to be misunderstandings and other conflicts. Given how common conflicts can be, it's important to know what to do when one arises. Ask clients if they have had recent or ongoing conflicts with important people in their lives. Have them think of what caused the conflict and how they handled it. Remind them that conflict can be overt (loud argument, slamming doors), indirect (withdrawing or refusing to speak to someone), or hidden (pretending that everything is okay, but showing anger in a passive aggressive or indirect way). The conflict might be with family or friends, but it could also be with medical providers, health insurance companies, or random people we encounter in day-to-day life. Questions to ask include the following:

- *What was the conflict about?*

- *How was the communication?*

- *How did each of you respond?*

- *Was there any sort of resolution? Why or why not?*

- *What would you have done differently?*

Tell clients that effective conflict resolution skills involve three key elements:

1. Assertiveness

2. Learning to fight "fair"

3. Negotiation

## Assertiveness

*Assertiveness* means being able to clearly and directly express our thoughts, feelings, and needs (our "rights") without violating the rights of others. Assertiveness is NOT being aggressive or attacking. Assertiveness is NOT being passive or withdrawn. No one is assertive 100% of the time, and we should "choose our battles" wisely. The key is to be able to be assertive and to know when to do it. This involves first caring about ourselves and recognizing our "rights" as human beings. Refer clients to the workbook for some general rights we sometimes forget.

Have clients assess whether assertiveness is difficult for them. If so, then have clients turn to the Promoting Assertiveness exercise in the workbook. In this exercise, clients will apply their newly acquired skills of balancing thoughts and using the A-B-C-D method to challenge beliefs about assertiveness that might get in the way. Clients can practice asserting themselves with you when settling on today's homework assignment and in setting the agenda for the next session. If assertiveness does not appear to be an issue, move on to the next section.

For clients near the end of life, assertiveness can be particularly challenging. As part of the progression of their disease, clients have most likely lost independence, control, and autonomy. Although basic needs like activities of daily living are met, clients may feel more reluctant to assert other needs (i.e., they already feel like a burden and don't want to ask for more). Friends and family might also start to infantilize the client (albeit with the best of intentions) and assume that they know what's best. It is important for both clients and caregivers to understand that the client is still an adult with adult needs regardless of her level of disability.

## Fighting Fair

Fighting (or conflict) is as inevitable as death and taxes. It's bound to happen to everyone at some time or another. The key is to learn the rules of constructive conflict that can help resolve the issue rather than making it worse. Unfair fighting can be attacking, hypercritical, loud, angry, unfocused, and sometimes violent, but unfair fighting can also be characterized by sulking, withdrawal, and passive-aggressive behavior. Refer to Table 8.1. for some common features of unfair fighting and constructive conflict.

The following questions might assist the client in understanding her fighting style and identifying areas for improvement. Although there may be overlap with her general style of communication, her fighting style may differ in important ways. Her responses should be compared to the examples in the table.

- *When was the last time you had a fight with someone?*

- *What happened? What were your thoughts, feelings, and behaviors?*

- *What was the other person's response? Were you satisfied? If not, what needed to happen?*

- *Was the problem an issue of communication? Listening or speaking?*

### Table 8.1 Features of Unfair Fighting and Constructive Conflict

| Unfair Fighting | Constructive Conflict |
| --- | --- |
| Bad timing-ambushed, too rushed, too many distractions | Setting a good time for both people |
| Blaming | Stating the specific issue at hand rather than jumping to blame |
| Too many issues from the past and present get brought up at once | Sticking to only one issue per conflict |
| Covering vulnerable feelings with anger or righteousness | Expressing the full range of one's emotions |
| Not hearing the other person | Active listening |
| Making impossible demands | Proposing specific changes |
| Threats and ultimatums | Describing consequences |
| Insults or "barbs" | Partnership, equality, and respect |
| Escalation | Taking time to cool off, staying focused |
| Sour endings or no resolution | Shared resolution or agreeing to disagree |

Adapted from McKay, Davis, & Fanning (2007).

■ *Was it a conflict of goals or needs? Expectations?*

■ *Did both of you follow the rules of constructive conflict? Was it unfair fighting?*

■ *What would you do differently if you could do it over?*

## Negotiation

The final set of skills needed for conflict resolution has to do with the art of negotiation, or what to do to find middle ground when each party has different and competing needs. Each negotiation has four potential stages. The client's approach to each of these stages will greatly influence both the outcome and the process of the negotiation. Even very difficult negotiations with very high stakes can be accomplished with respect and partnership.

1. *Preparation:* Before talking about the problem, know how you feel and what you want. What are acceptable outcomes? Where can

you bend? Remember that flexibility is a key skill, but so is assertiveness and knowing what you need.

2. *Discussion:* Both parties describe the facts of the situation and provide information. You need to understand the other person's reasoning and feelings and vice versa.

3. *Proposal and counterproposal:* Both parties make offers and look for common ground. You will have to adapt and change your offers as needed.

4. *Agreement and disagreement:* Is there enough common ground? Have you planned on a course of action? Have you "agreed to disagree?"

Tell the client that the following negotiation tips might be helpful the next time conflict arises.

1. Understand and manage your feelings. Perfectly good and reasonable people can have differing opinions and needs. Are you experiencing strong emotions? Why? What are the actual stakes involved? Do a little soul searching if you get stuck or overwhelmed.

2. Separate the people from the problem. It doesn't have to be about personalities. Most people have the same general goals (e.g., to be happy, loved, successful) but may have different ideas of how to go about achieving them.

3. Express empathy and sensitivity. Everyone needs to feel heard, even if you don't agree with them and can't give them what they want. Try to understand the person. Empathy, active listening, and emotional honesty are all essential.

4. State your interests or motivations as a way to find common ground. Maybe your motivations are in line but your methods are different.

5. Have a "BATNA," or Best Alternative To a Negotiated Agreement. If you can't get exactly what you want, what is a good Plan B?

6. Try to be flexible. Brainstorm alternatives together. What can each of you live with?

7.  Give a little to get a little. "Giving in" this time might help you the next time around.

8.  If things get too heated or too stuck, postpone negotiations.

9.  Share positive feedback and appreciation after you've reached an agreement.

## Caring for One's Relationships: Quality Time

Conflict resolution becomes a much easier proposition within the context of a strong relationship. It is important to remember that relationships need attention even when there isn't anything to be fixed.

Explain that an important part of relationship strengthening includes spending "quality time" together. Even when we're healthy this can sometimes be a challenge. When we're ill, the competing demands of doctor's appointments, medication side effects, limited mobility, etc. can all make quality time seem almost nonexistent.

Ask clients for some examples of quality time they've spent with family or friends recently. Discuss how this is different from when they weren't ill and any changes that they would like to make. Refer them to the workbook for a partial list of shared activities that other patients have tried and enjoyed in the past. Remind participants that these activities can strengthen their relationships and they can also help them both feel less depressed and anxious.

## Getting the Most out of Health Care

## Getting the Most from Health Care Providers

Ask your client to name her primary doctor and any other important physicians or health care providers. In order to best work with this team, it is important to be able to name all members and understand their roles. Refer the patient to the workbook form My Health Care Team.

On their own time, clients should complete this team listing, including contact information and role descriptions.

Ask clients to recall one positive and one negative example of a relationship with a health care provider. What made the positive relationship work? What made the negative one so bad? Although physicians and other health care providers are in positions of power and treatment authority, they are first and foremost human beings—in both good ways and bad. The following list of suggestions (also listed in the workbook) can assist the client in nurturing a positive relationship with a health care provider. You may want to use the sample dialogues in your discussion.

1. Develop an empathic understanding of what your doctor does.

   *Your doctor probably seems rushed. She may seem abrupt, distracted, uninterested, or even short-tempered. It is important to remember that your doctor may have been up all night, may have dozens of very complex (and very upset) patients in just one day, or may have personal problems of her own. There are a million and one high-stress things for her to do, and pressures from health insurers are only getting worse and worse. Although this isn't an excuse, it is a reason to not take her response personally. If it seems right, give her a second chance before moving on to someone else (assuming you have a choice). If you don't have a choice, express some empathy but let her know how you are feeling—e.g., "Doc, I'm sorry things are so busy and stressful around here, but I'm really counting on you to hear what I have to say. . . ."*

2. Remember that your doctor is just a person.

   *Doctors make mistakes. They have bad days. They may get cranky or annoyed. You might remind them of a family member they lost, or the issue you have might cause them some embarrassment. Your doctor may also be someone substantially younger and less experienced in life than you. Although doctors may have "heard it all," they still have emotional reactions, no matter how good their poker faces might be. Although being human means making mistakes, it also means being capable of learning and growing. Your physician may grow with you or perhaps because of you. Don't be intimidated. Your doctor is human too.*

3.  Give positive feedback.

    *Most doctors are critical and perfectionistic by nature. They worry that they have missed something or feel like they are a step behind in keeping up with all the latest medical advances. Let you doctor know when she does something right, says something meaningful, or provides good service.*

4.  Although doctors are pressed to be efficient, don't be afraid to be yourself.

    *When appropriate, share information about your life, your family, or things that make you a unique individual. Most doctors won't have much time for this kind of exchange, but when the opportunity arises, take it. It is much more rewarding to care for a person than to care for a body with a disease.*

## Getting the Most out of Doctor's Visits

Remind the client that she is a partner in her health care. She gets a "vote" and may provide important information for diagnosis or management. However, being a partner also means that the client (and/or a caregiver) has the responsibility to prepare before a doctor's appointment. If clients are not sure what would be most helpful, they should ask their doctors. Some ways to prepare include bringing a list of current medications with dosages and frequencies (or the pill bottles), bringing a list of the most important things the patient would like to discuss in that visit, and doing any "homework" that might have been assigned (e.g., recording blood sugar levels, tracking frequency of certain symptoms). Other suggestions include the following. You may want to use the sample dialogues in your discussion.

1.  Know your medical history.

    *It will save a lot of time if you can bring a medical summary or copies of past medical records. Bring information on your family's medical history too. Be sure to include a record of past medications and medical tests that you may have already tried (rather than reinventing the wheel with each new doctor).*

2.  Ask questions and take notes.

    *If you tend to forget what you need to ask when you are in the appointment, write down the most important questions and bring them with you to the visit. Don't be afraid to jot down questions or other notes while your doctor is talking (she probably takes notes while you are talking too). You might also want to bring a friend or family member to help you recall what was said or you could tape record the visit. A lot might get said in those 15 minutes!*

3.  Express how you feel.

    *Your doctor isn't a mind reader. She may not know you well enough to read your emotional signals or she may be too distracted to catch your emotional clues. If you are afraid, angry, or sad, let her know about it. Practice your new communication skills.*

4.  Summarize the visit.

    *Before your doctor ends the visit and walks out the door, be sure to attempt a summary of what was discussed in the visit and what you are now supposed to do. This helps the doctor and you see how well you communicated with one another, clarifies any changes to the treatment plan, and reminds both of you what needs to be done before the next visit.*

5.  Ask for other help.

    *If you run out of time but need more information about your disease, treatments, or testing, ask if there is another health care team member who can help out. Doctors can often refer you to a health educator, nurse, or behavioral medicine specialist with expertise in chronic disease management.*

## How to Communicate with a Doctor's Answering Service

Remind clients that often the most challenging (and frightening) times are when urgent medical issues emerge during evening or weekend hours when the doctor's office is closed. They can greatly alleviate anxiety and facilitate the process of getting help if they follow a few simple steps. You may want to review your own after-hours contact policy as an example.

1. During regular working hours, ask staff at your medical clinic about their procedures for after-hours coverage. All clinics have an answering service with an on-call system or some agreement with a local hospital that can provide urgent or emergency medical care. Keep these after-hours contact numbers posted in several places in your house—e.g., by the phone, on the refrigerator, etc.

2. If you have a special agreement with your doctor (e.g., an unusually high but needed dose of pain meds), be sure your doctor makes a note in your medical chart. The on-call doctor may not be familiar with your case and the note can save a great deal of time and frustration.

3. Before making the after-hours call, jot down a few notes about what happened and why you are calling. It is easy to get flustered on an after-hours call and forget to share critical information. Before calling, you should make sure that this is not an issue that could wait until the morning.

4. If you get an answering service (and not a qualified medical professional), leave the important information, including a call-back number. If it is not a life-or-death situation, allow your doctor 30 minutes to get back to you before calling again. If you call back, verify that the answering service has the correct information and call-back number.

5. When the doctor calls you back, remember that you might not get your regular doctor. Doctors usually take turns providing after-hours coverage. This new doctor may not have your medical chart and may not be aware of any of your medications or other arrangements you might have made with your regular doctor.

6. If you are having a medical emergency such as chest pain, take steps to get yourself to an emergency room unless you and your doctor have already come up with another plan (e.g., take a nitro pill or aspirin then wait a few minutes).

7.  Remember to not be afraid to assert yourself—the "squeaky wheel" does often get the oil. However, a little etiquette can often accomplish your goals more effectively without wasting your energy on anger.

## Homework

✎ Have client complete the My Ways of Communicating form.

✎ Have client complete the My Communication Family Tree Form and answer reflection questions (optional).

✎ Have client complete the Promoting Assertiveness Form.

✎ Have client practice communication or conflict skills with a friend or family member.

✎ Have client schedule a quality-time activity with a friend or family member.

✎ Have client complete the My Health Care Team form.

## FAQs from Clients

1.  All of these structured communication steps don't seem right to me. They just don't match my style. Don't I have to be true to myself instead of pretending to be someone else?

    *A: Yes, of course you need to be true to yourself. Ask yourself how well your current communication style works for you. How healthy are your current relationships? Do you get your needs met? Do you often have conflict? If it looks like there might be room for improvement, think about some changes you might try that will still fit your style. The suggestions are just suggestions and not steadfast rules. Feel free to adapt them but be sure to test out any changes you make.*

2.  I can learn all I want about how to fight fair, but if my partner isn't following the rules, too, then what am I supposed to do?

*A: It is important for both people to fight fair. However, one partner can take the lead and set an example of how to be effective at conflict resolution. You can still assert yourself by telling your partner how his unfair tactics make you feel and how they affect the resolution. You may still reach an impasse and need to postpone any resolution or seek out a third party arbitrator such as a counselor or therapist.*

3. I was taught to keep a stiff upper lip. You are not supposed to complain or "assert" yourself. You are not supposed to be in conflict. All that talk about "rights" makes me feel too uppity or conceited.

   *A: Many people have been taught to suppress their feelings and avoid conflict at all costs. If this approach is accepted by your family and seems to be effective, you may not need to make any major adjustments. However, if this style has caused some problems or has possibly limited how close you might become to others, consider a few first steps you might try out. It is not all black or white—all suppression or all expression. Evaluate and adjust as needed.*

# Module 4
## Quality of Life

# Session 9 — *Management of Medical Symptoms*

*(Corresponds to session 9 of the workbook)*

## Materials Needed

- Flip chart or board
- Symptom Management Worksheet
- My Pain Diary form
- My Pain Management Plan form
- My Pain Panic Plan form

## Outline

- Set agenda
- Review homework
- Discuss how to manage medical symptoms
- Give tips for coping with chronic pain
- Give tips for coping with insomnia or sleep problems
- Give tips for coping with other common medical symptoms
- Close discussion on symptom management
- Assign homework

### Facilitator Note

*As always, clients should consult with their physicians before making any changes to their medical care. Encourage clients to first talk with their physician before trying any of the strategies discussed in this session. Clients may want to use this session to develop ideas, then run those ideas by the medical team. Ideally, clients will have an appointment to see their physician shortly after this session.*

## Setting the Agenda

Set the agenda by referring to the session outline. At this point in the treatment program, clients should be taking more of an active role in setting the agenda. They should expect to begin each session with agenda setting and should know that homework review will always be an agenda item. Hopefully, they will be thinking about items to add to the agenda. If they are not at this point, encourage them to bring in an agenda item for next time or ask them to think of any recent personal events or examples related to today's agenda.

## Homework Review

Review the homework from the last session. Identify any obstacles to completing homework and problem solve as needed. Remind the client that homework is key to getting the most out of the program. If there have been any problems with completing homework, use this situation as an active opportunity for the client to practice his newly acquired communication and problem-solving skills. These same skills may be essential when negotiating a new symptom management plan with his medical doctor following this session.

## Managing Medical Symptoms

There is no easy way to live with pain, shortness of breath, insomnia, nausea, or any of the other difficult medical symptoms or treatment side effects that often accompany serious medical illnesses. Medications, physical therapy, certain exercises, diet, and other healthy behaviors can help, but sometimes the symptoms just won't go away. Although symptom management has traditionally been seen as the responsibility of the physician, newer models of chronic disease management emphasize the importance of client participation and engagement (Bodenheimer, Lorig, Halstead, & Grumbach, 2002). In fact, some argue that the physician is simply the "coach" and the client is the "star player" most responsible for success. Although the initial game plan (i.e., medications, surgeries, etc.) is determined by the physician, it is the client who must implement and follow these instructions in addition to other self-selected strategies and modifications that ultimately contribute to effective symptom management.

Before the end of this session, the client should identify at least one key symptom or side effect he would like to manage and one possible intervention he can realistically implement. It is important to design a "success experience"—i.e., break down symptom management and select a small piece that is easy to achieve so the client can begin building self-confidence and motivation to do more. A first step might include cutting out caffeine after 2 pm (for insomnia), taking a hot bath every night (for muscle soreness), or finding a list of local medical massage therapists. Regardless of the symptom chosen, the homework will probably require three skills learned in earlier sessions—goal setting, self-monitoring, and problem solving. Ultimately, any new strategies should be integrated into a more comprehensive treatment plan including those interventions selected by the client's physician.

Present the following problem-solving steps adapted for symptom management.

## Step 1: Get the Right Attitude

Clients are probably not new to the idea of symptom self-management. They may have a long history of successes and failures. Remind clients that they are the "star players" and they need to step up to manage their disease whenever possible. Even if they have been unsuccessful in the past, new attempts bring new opportunities for success. If they remain skeptical, encourage them to try out an option before discounting it.

## Step 2: Identify the Problem and Think about Your Goals

Discuss the client's current medical symptoms and management strategies. Are these strategies effective? What are the management goals and have they been met? Ask clients about their symptoms (i.e., problems), priorities, and desired outcomes. Use the following questions to begin filling out the Symptom Management Worksheet (in workbook):

■ *What symptoms (or side effects) do you have that are most troubling?*

■ *If you could pick only one symptom to change, what would it be?*

■ *What would you like to see happen with this symptom?*

Emphasize that it is important to keep the goal small and keep it specific (refer to the results of the initial intake assessment and the preliminary goals set in Session 1). For example, rather than having the goal "I want my leg to be pain-free," a better goal would be "I would like to manage my leg pain enough to allow me to walk down the stairs and out of my apartment once a day." Stress that small goals do not mean giving up hope but do require breaking a daunting task into small, achievable pieces. ("Every journey begins with one step."). Ask the client to write his first goal in the Symptom Management Worksheet.

## Step 3: List Specific Options to Achieve Your Goal

The next step is to gather information about the target symptom and think of specific medical and nonmedical interventions that can help achieve the goal. Self-monitoring might be used to gather information on the symptom (e.g., intensity, frequency, triggers, etc.). Also remind the client to use the steps of problem solving in Session 3. This session will discuss specific suggestions to address the most common medical symptoms and side effects. Clients should test out one strategy then evaluate its effectiveness. If it doesn't work, there are almost always other strategies to try. Encourage clients to list initial ideas on the Symptom Management Worksheet. This record of symptom interventions may prove valuable for the client, caregivers, and the medical or hospice team.

### Step 4: Choose the Best Option

Recall the process of choosing the best option in Session 3. Clients may want to turn to the Pick an Option Form from that session. Of the options listed, clients should consider the pros and cons of each choice, the impact on self and others, and the probability of goal achievement.

### Step 5: Implement the Option and Evaluate the Outcome

After the best option has been selected, the client should develop an implementation plan—i.e., when, where, and how to start trying the new strategy. A self-monitoring plan should be in place to evaluate the impact of this new intervention—e.g., ongoing sleep diary, pain ratings, etc. See the discussion of specific symptoms next for more detailed examples.

## Chronic Pain

If relevant to the client, discuss how chronic pain can be one of the most debilitating and demoralizing of serious medical symptoms. It's hard to think, it's hard to act, it's hard to do anything if a nagging (or screaming) pain is always present. Medications can help and should be used as prescribed, but they can have side effects and they're not always 100% effective. Since pain may vary from day to day, management strategies need to have some flexibility.

First explain what is meant by pain. Pain has two components that both respond to medical and nonmedical interventions. To best manage the pain, the client should have interventions that address each component.

$$\text{Pain} = \text{Physical Sensation} + \text{Emotional Suffering}$$

## Physical Sensation

Undoubtedly, there's a physical component to pain. Nerves send pain messages to the brain, indicating something is injured or just not quite right. The acute pain signal is meant to convey important information about something going on in the body so the person can do something about it. However, the physical pain sensation can also be chronic (i.e., from an "injury" that can't be repaired) or it can be a false alarm caused by nerve misfiring or the brain misreading signals as pain (e.g., as in fibromyalgia, phantom limb pain, etc). The physical sensation can come and go, sometimes with no predictable reason. It can be described with different qualities such as sharp, burning, throbbing, or aching.

In the medical profession, pain is now considered the "fifth vital sign" along with pulse, temperature, respiration, and blood pressure. Most medical providers will do a brief assessment of physical sensations of pain. They may ask the client to rate the intensity of pain on a scale of 1–10 both for the present moment but also as an average over the past week. This type of numeric rating is a useful way to set a pain baseline and to later assess the impact of any pain interventions. The client may also be asked a standard set of questions to assist the provider in understanding the cause and treatment of his pain. These questions might include the following:

- Where is the pain? (Location)

- When did the pain start? (Onset)

- How often does the pain occur? (Frequency)

- What does the pain feel like? (Quality)

- Has pain intensity changed? (Duration, Variability, Temporality)

- Is there anything that makes the pain better or worse? (Variability, Responsivity)

A large variety of different pain medications can help dull or perhaps totally eliminate the physical sensation of pain. It may take several attempts before the right medication and dosage are found. There are also a number of non-medication interventions that might help reduce the physical sensations of pain. Each client should work closely with his primary care provider or a pain clinic to develop a comprehensive pain management plan based on what works best for that client's particular pain. Clients can start by using their self-monitoring skills to rate their pain and other important factors on a regular basis (see Pain Diary in workbook). After selecting and implementing a new pain intervention, clients can re-rate the intensity and quality of their pain.

Nonpharmacologic interventions might include the following:

- Physical therapy (stretching, exercises)

- Hydrotherapy or spa treatments, hot showers or baths

- Electrotherapy or transcutaneous electrical nerve stimulation

- Ultrasound

- Acupuncture or acupressure

- Massage (done by a professional or layperson; massage chairs or pads)

- Walking aids (e.g., crutches, insoles, braces)

- Supportive devices (e.g., pillows, bandages, sling)

- Therapeutic heat and cold (e.g., heating pad, ice packs)

- Soothing or hot creams (e.g., Icy Hot, Ben Gay, capsaicin ointments)

- Progressive muscle relaxation to reduce muscle tension

- Physical exercise

- Weight loss

- Yoga

- Nutritional changes

## Emotional Suffering or Distress

The physical sensation of pain is only half the equation—and sometimes it is the easiest half to manage. The other half of the equation is the emotional suffering or distress tied to the experience of being in pain. It's important to remember that pain is stressful and chronic pain means chronic stress. Other sessions have already discussed the links between stress and physical well-being. Remind the client that one's attitude or how one thinks about pain can directly influence the intensity of one's pain or suffering. Depression, anxiety, and hopelessness all make the experience of pain far worse. Refer the client to the sessions on dealing with stress, depression, and anxiety if these seem to be factors contributing to the client's emotional suffering. Present the following suggestions as additional ways to reduce the emotional suffering component of pain. Remind clients that "pain may be mandatory but suffering is negotiable."

### Ways to Reduce the Emotional Distress Component of Pain

- Deep breathing to reduce anxiety and tension

- Massage (the intimacy and support can also ease emotional suffering)

- Relaxation tapes

- Mindfulness—either meditation or developing the habit of being present to all that is around you

- Self-hypnosis

- Music—for relaxation or distraction

- Problem solving—provides a sense of control, mastery, and hope

- Biofeedback

- Mental imagery

- Pacing, time management

- Self-talk—affirmations, reframing, balancing thoughts, A-B-C-D exercises, etc.

- Distraction—e.g., TV, talking to friends, hobbies

- Support or therapy groups

- Individual therapy or counseling

- Social support

- Humor

With the help of a primary care provider or pain specialist, clients should be able to come up with a pain plan that includes pharmacologic and nonpharmacologic strategies to be used on a regular basis. Clients should also have a "panic plan" that includes what they should do if they have serious breakthrough pain. Stress to the client that pain can and should be controlled. If pain is an issue for your client, walk them through the Pain Diary, Pain Management Plan, and Pain Panic Plan forms in the workbook. Caregivers and medical providers might need to assist the patient in completing these forms.

## Insomnia or Sleep Problems

Difficulty sleeping can be a very common and troubling consequence of medical illness. Explain to the client that insomnia can include trouble falling asleep, trouble staying asleep, or waking up too early. Insomnia can be caused by many different things, including chronic pain, worry or anxiety, depression, taking too many naps during the day, alcohol use, caffeine or other stimulants, staying up too late, lack of exercise, sleep apnea or other trouble breathing, not keeping a regular sleep schedule, side effects of certain medications, and other causes. Although it is not always possible to determine the cause of the sleep problems, some exploration might help clients select the most helpful interventions.

Treatments for insomnia fall into two categories, medication and cognitive-behavioral interventions.

## Medication

Medications for insomnia can include sleeping pills (i.e., sedatives), pain pills, and psychiatric medications such as antidepressants. In general, sleeping pills are considered a short-term fix, since most of them have side effects and some can be habit forming. However, sleeping pills can be very useful if a client is facing a particularly tough time or if all other insomnia treatment options have been exhausted. It is important that sleeping pills not be used as a way to escape from depression or pain, although they can be used in addition to medications for these problems.

Since pain is a common cause of insomnia, getting better pain control through better pain management is often a good solution. For some clients, pain medications also have the side effect of sedation, which can be beneficial when taken before bedtime. Clients should make sure their pain management has been optimized before adding new medications to make them sleep.

Depression and anxiety are also common causes of insomnia, and both can be treated with medications. Because of the drowsiness side effect of many antidepressants, they may be prescribed to help with sleep even if the client does not meet criteria for depression (e.g., trazodone). Unlike many sleeping pills, these antidepressants do not carry the risk of physiologic dependence. Many physicians will first try an antidepressant sleep aid before moving to sleeping pills.

If your client has notable insomnia, ask him to list the medications he currently uses to help him sleep. Does the client know what category these drugs fall into? Does he know how he should take these medications? Ask the client to write down any questions he might have about sleep medications for his next doctor's appointment.

## Cognitive-Behavioral Interventions for Sleep

There are a number of non-medication ways to improve sleep. In fact, recent research has shown that these changes in behavior and thinking work just as well or better than sleeping pills, although they may take more effort and patience (Sivertsen et al., 2006). Following are some suggestions commonly called "sleep hygiene."

*CAFFEINE:* This stimulant is found in coffee, tea, some sodas, and even some over-the-counter medications (like Excedrin). Try not to have any caffeine after lunchtime. Remember that even though you might be able to fall asleep after having caffeine, it might still be interfering with your quality of sleep (i.e., you can't get to the deeper, more restful stages of sleep).

*SUGAR:* Some people can be very sensitive to sugar (like sweets, candies, etc.). Try not to have any sugar or sweets close to bedtime (at least 2–3 hours before bed should be sugar-free).

*FLUIDS:* Limit your fluid intake several hours before bedtime to avoid late night trips to the bathroom.

*NAPS:* Many people can fall asleep for short periods of time during the day. Naps can feel satisfying or refreshing, but can greatly interfere with your ability to sleep at night. Do not take daytime naps. If you must nap, limit yourself to a 1-hour nap near lunchtime.

*EXERCISE:* If your physical health permits, regular exercise may deepen your sleep. Do not exercise within a few hours of sleep.

*CONSISTENT SLEEP SCHEDULE:* Varying the time you get up can negatively affect your sleep. It is especially important to get up at the same time every day—even on the weekends—regardless of how well you slept.

*BEDTIME:* Only go to bed when you feel sleepy. Tossing and turning in bed can cause you to associate your bed with frustration and wakefulness.

*WAKING UP:* Many people wake up in the middle of the night (or much too early) and can't get back to sleep. If this happens to you, try to relax and fall back to sleep. If you cannot fall back to sleep within 15–25 minutes, get out of bed and do something in another room. Return to bed only when you begin to feel sleepy again.

*BED:* It is important not to use your bed for reading, watching TV, or other activities. Use your bed only for sleep or sex.

*CLOCK WATCHING:* If you tend to look at the clock every few minutes, turn it around or cover it up. Looking at it only makes you more anxious.

*THOUGHTS:* Don't get mad at yourself for not being able to fall asleep. Insomnia is a very common condition. Remind yourself that insomnia cannot last forever (even though it seems that way) and insomnia cannot kill you. Remind yourself that there are things you can do to make it better. Eventually, your mind and body will force you to go to sleep. Use your newly acquired thought-balancing or A-B-C-D skills if needed.

*SNORING:* If you wake yourself up snoring and find you can sleep better on your side, sew a pocket onto the back of your pajama top and insert a tennis ball. This keeps you from rolling on your back in the middle of the night.

*BEDTIME RITUAL:* Sometimes a relaxing nighttime routine can get you ready for sleep. Try a glass of warm milk, a warm bath, a back-rub, soothing music, or reading a relaxing book.

*SLEEP ENVIRONMENT:* Make sure your sleep environment is conducive to sleep—i.e., maintain quiet (maybe use masking "white noise" such as a fan), keep at a comfortable temperature (not too hot or cold), have fresh sheets, etc.

If insomnia is an issue for clients, remind them to use the skills of self-monitoring and problem solving. Assist clients in creating a sleep diary that captures sleep quantity, sleep quality, daytime fatigue, daytime naps, and other factors deemed important. As clients try new sleep interventions, they should monitor and evaluate any sleep changes. The creation of this new diary is an important step in helping clients learn how to develop their own forms and exercises in the future.

## Dealing with Other Common Symptoms

The following are other common symptoms and management suggestions offered by hospice and other palliative care providers (e.g., Lynn & Harrold, 1999; McFarlane & Bashe, 1988). While some suggestions are evidence based, others are drawn from clinical experience or trial and error. All clients should notify their doctor of any management suggestions they would like to implement. Remind clients that for each symptom, they should follow the structured steps of problem solving. The following lists are intended as possible options to be used in this problem-solving process. All symptoms may be worked through on the Symptom Management Worksheet or similar form created by the client.

## Nausea (Feeling Sick to Your Stomach)

1. Eat salty and bland foods such as dry toast and crackers (unless a salt-restricted diet has been recommended).

2. Eat small, frequent meals and snack at bedtime.

3. Eat only foods you like and foods that smell pleasant.

4. Eat food cold or at room temperature so it has less taste and smell.

5. Sip all liquids and eat foods slowly.

6. Try a liquid calorie supplement such as Ensure.

7. Report nausea to your doctor and take medications as prescribed.

8. Rest for at least 1 hour after each meal.

9. Relax, take deep breaths, distract yourself with TV, etc.

10. Don't force food or liquids if you're feeling nauseated.

11. Try ice chips or popsicles if drinking liquid is too much.

12. Take all pills with a lot of liquid (unless otherwise indicated).

## Dry Mouth

1. Drink plenty of fluids (unless you have been instructed to limit fluid intake). Always keep a bottle of water with you.

2. Drink fluids with meals to moisten food and help swallowing.

3. Use ice chips, hard sugarless candies, frozen grapes, or sugarless gum to stimulate saliva production.

4. Add liquids to solid food (e.g., sauces, gravy, yogurt).

5. Keep lips moist (if you are on oxygen, petroleum jelly is not recommended).

6. Use good mouth care (brushing, flossing, mouth rinses).

7. Avoid spicy, hot, or acidic foods.

8. Avoid foods that require a lot of chewing.

9. Use artificial saliva (available over the counter).

## Constipation

1. Increase use of high-fiber foods such as bran, wheat germ, raw fruits and vegetables, juices, dates, prunes, etc. or take over-the-counter fiber supplements.

2. Increase fluid intake unless otherwise instructed by your doctor.

3. Increase physical activity as much as possible (e.g., walking).

4. Use laxatives or stool softeners as directed, but remember that regular reliance on them might cause problems later.

5. Avoid foods that cause constipation such as cheese, eggs, bananas, etc.

6. Remember that you don't have to have a bowel movement every day. Once every few days is okay.

7. Don't overstrain yourself trying to move your bowels. Try to create a regular schedule but accept that some days it might not work.

## Swelling in Arms, Legs, Hands, and Feet (Edema)

1. When sitting in a chair, keep feet elevated.

2. Rest in bed with the swollen part elevated above heart level.

3. Eat as well as you can, especially foods high in protein.

4. Take medications as prescribed (these might include diuretics or "water pills").

5. Ask the doctor if you should modify your diet.

6. Sometimes stockings or other supportive garments can help. Ask your doctor.

## Shortness of Breath

1. Remain calm. Shortness of breath is common and usually passes quickly if caused by overexertion. When your body relaxes, it needs less oxygen.

2. Sit upright in chair or raise your head with pillows (do not lie flat).

3. Take medications or treatments prescribed for the problem such as oxygen or inhalers.

4. Inhale through your nose and exhale through pursed lips.

5. If spitting up mucus note the amount, the color, (normal is clear or white), and if there is an odor.

## Closing Discussion

Tell the client that all of these practical tips can go a long way toward managing medical symptoms. However, in order for them to work their best, it is important for the client to be in the right frame of mind. Sometimes feeling stressed, nervous, or depressed can make physical symptoms much worse. Remind clients to use their skills for stress management and coping with depression and anxiety. They can refer back to the corresponding chapters in the workbook or bring it up as an additional agenda item to be discussed in future sessions. Also remind clients to share these notes with their caregivers. Caregivers could use some advice on helping clients manage symptoms, too.

## Homework

✎ Have client consult with his medical team about trying out new symptom management strategies.

✎ Have client complete Symptom Management Worksheet.

✎ Have client complete My Pain Diary (if relevant).

✎ Have client complete My Pain Management Plan (if relevant).

✎ Have client complete My Pain Panic Plan (if relevant)

✎ Have client create and use sleep diary (if relevant).

## FAQs from Clients

1. It seems like whenever I do something to manage one symptom, it makes another symptom worse or creates an entirely new problem

(e.g., taking more pain meds makes me constipated). It seems like I just can't win.

*A: All medications do have side effects, although some are worse than others. As part of your problem-solving process, you have to evaluate which is the lesser of two evils—the original symptom or the side effect of the new treatment. It is important to remember, too, that there are often a number of other options that might not have side effects—either different medications or non-medication interventions. Don't give up hope. Keep trying.*

2. I would like to be the "star player on the team" but my doctor doesn't seem interested in letting me try my own symptom management ideas. How can I problem solve if he won't let me make any changes?

*A: Be sure you understand why your doctor might be having reservations. He might be worried about a particular strategy you want to try or he might have had a bad experience in the past that he is afraid you will repeat. See if he is opposed to the general idea of a partnership with you. If he is opposed to teamwork and you would like to be on a team, it might be time to find a new doctor. If he likes the idea of a team but just doesn't have the time, see if you can discuss your management ideas with a nurse or behavioral medicine specialist.*

3. I'm doing everything I can to manage my pain, but it still feels out of control. When I tell my doctor about it, he seems like he doesn't believe me. I feel like a drug addict asking for more pills but I'm desperate for relief!

*A: No one deserves to be in pain. There are wide variety of effective pain medications and nonpharmacological interventions. If your doctor is not willing to help you create a comprehensive and effective pain management program, ask for a referral to a pain management clinic. If that is not possible, find a new doctor who will treat your pain.*

# Session 10 *Quality of Life: Setting Goals and Looking Forward*

*(Corresponds to session 10 of the workbook)*

## Materials Needed

- Flip chart or board
- My Quality of Life (QOL) Worksheet
- Goals of the Day form
- My Quality of Life Goals form

## Outline

- Set agenda
- Review homework
- Introduce palliative care and hospice
- Discuss quality of life (QOL) construct
- Help client set QOL goals
- Discuss how to achieve goals
- Review medical goals including advanced directives
- Have the client consider doing an end-of-life or legacy project
- Prepare client for upcoming end of the program

## Setting the Agenda

Set the agenda by referring to the session outline. At this point in the treatment program, clients should be taking more of an active role in setting the agenda and adding their own items. It is critical that the last agenda item regarding the end of the program be discussed. Clients will need to do extra preparation for their last session, and a number of issues around endings may emerge.

## Homework Review

Review the homework from the last session. Identify any obstacles to completing homework and problem solve as needed. Since the homework was a first step in trying new symptom management techniques, have clients assign themselves other steps for the upcoming weeks and months.

## Introduction to Palliative Care and Hospice

The fields of geriatrics, palliative care, and the broader hospice movement are nothing short of a revolution for medicine. Disability, serious illness, and death and dying have been brought out of the closet and into mainstream. In these fields, decline and death are seen as natural stages of life worthy of as much attention as any other stage. With this attention comes the recognition that the current focus on quantity of life (by many oncologists, surgeons, etc.) is well intentioned but unidimensional and sometimes even harmful. We fail our clients and ourselves when quantity of life is emphasized and quality of life is ignored. By attending to the emotional, social, and spiritual needs of clients nearing the end of life, we may greatly affect quality. Sometimes the "successful" outcome is in facilitating a "good death."

Introduce clients to the perspectives behind palliative and hospice care. Emphasize the focus on quality of life, however it may be uniquely defined for each client. Many clients may have the mistaken impression that hospice means inpatient hospitalization, "banishment" to a nursing home for the dying, or being surrounded by crunchy, new-age harpists who force them to give up on life and "let go." In reality, there are many levels of hospice care, starting with a very basic, one-time palliative care consultation directed at improving comfort and quality of life. Stress to the client that accepting palliative care does not necessarily mean giving up on curative care. The following exploration of quality of life should assist clients in defining the construct for themselves, setting goals, and considering future interventions to achieve those goals.

## Quality of Life (QOL)

What is meant by "quality of life?" There is currently no consensus on the official definition of this important construct, however, it is quickly becoming a focus in health-related research when measuring the impact of medical interventions. It is typically thought to have several elements, including functionality (physical ability, ability to work, ability to care for self, etc.), mental health, social relationships, and spirituality. These categories are differentially weighted depending on the values and preferences of the client. It is recognized that client values may change over time—e.g., impairments in functionality may initially cause large drops in perceived quality of life, but these impairments matter less as the client adapts and comes to value other elements more.

Considerable time, energy, and money are spent on the treatment of symptoms and disease as a way to improve QOL. However, it would be a mistake to focus only on eradication of the negative. While addressing negative aspects one can also incorporate interventions to build positive ones—i.e., to bolster strengths, support growth, and generally improve one's quality of life. The burgeoning field of "positive psychology" aims to identify and promote empirically supported interventions to achieve these goals (Seligman, Steen, Park, & Peterson, 2005). Encourage clients to expand their thinking about QOL to include addressing both positive and negative aspects. Specific recommendations from positive psychology are included in the final section of this chapter.

Ask clients to turn to the Quality of Life (QOL) exercise in the workbook. Clients will begin developing their personal definition of QOL—i.e., a list of important components, what those components include, and their relative weights. After discussion of how they have defined quality of life, clients should make an initial rating of their quality of life using the QOL Visual Analog Scale in the workbook. Clients will later set goals to improve or maintain their quality of life. Although some aspects of QOL may be beyond the client's control, it is important to emphasize that there is always some percentage that can be controlled. For uncontrollable impacts on QOL, clients should refer back to Session 3 on coping skills (i.e., emotion-focused coping) or Session 11 on resilience and transcendence.

## Goal Setting for Improved Quality of Life

Given that diseases, treatments, and social circumstances are nearly always changing, the goal of maximizing QOL has to be an ongoing effort. Emphasize to the client that just because she is seriously ill doesn't mean she has to give up living and growing. In fact, illness can sometimes help us grow faster and grow further than if we'd stayed healthy. To keep some sense of direction and purpose and have something to look forward to, recommend that the client set some specific and realistic long-term and short-term goals related to QOL. Start with short-term goals by asking the client what her goals are for today. Remind the client to keep goals very specific and realistic. For example, a goal of "being happy" is a bit vague and gives no idea about how to achieve it. A goal of "visiting my granddaughter after this session and sharing old stories" is specific and realistic, and can make a person happy. Encourage clients to try to make a "goal of the day" every morning for the next week or two. They should note how this affects the way they feel and their sense of accomplishment. Refer clients to the example goals included in the corresponding workbook chapter and to the Pleasant Activities List in Session 4. They can also refer to Sessions 7 and 8 for goals involving social support and building intimacy.

Clients should also set larger QOL goals for the week, the month, or the year. While there's no guarantee they'll be able to finish these projects, there's no reason why they can't at least start them and enjoy the process. Tell participants that goals can refer to material changes, personal growth, relationships, enjoyment, business, health, lifestyle, etc. Refer to the initial goals clients set in Session 1. Do these goals still fit? Have clients elaborate or change these medium to longer term goals using the My Quality of Life Goals form in the workbook. Examples of long-term goals are included on the form to help clients get started. Remind clients that the overall goal is to improve QOL in whatever way they define it.

## Achieving Quality of Life Goals

After the client has written down some initial goals in her workbook, elicit a general sense of how confident the client is in her ability to achieve those goals. If confidence is low (but goals are realistic), she may need some help building self-efficacy. Have the client recall past experiences of success, list available resources, share inspirational success stories from other patients, and problem solve around any anticipated obstacles. Remind the client of the affirmations of her positive qualities and signature strengths generated in Session 2. It is helpful for clients to revisit this list often and consider how those qualities or strengths may be put into action. Clients will have an opportunity to revise and discuss QOL goals during the final session.

Tell the client that thinking of and setting QOL goals is half the battle; the second half is finding a way to achieve goals despite the inevitable difficulties that will arise. Review pointers from Session 3 on problem solving. Emphasize that sometimes a little brainstorming and early preparations can go a long way. Also offer a few other suggestions:

- Break your goals down into small, easy steps (i.e., graded task assignment)

- If you have thoughts that discourage you, do an A-B-C-D exercise

- Mark and recognize your progress each step of the way (progress may be partial achievement of the goal or it may be any impact on QOL)

- Remember that no one achieves 100% of their goals 100% of the time

- Make sure goals are realistic and key resources are available

- Allow yourself to work at your own speed—sometimes a leisurely pace improves quality of life

- View obstacles or setbacks as a challenge

- Don't be afraid to ask for support or help when you need it (refer to Session 7)

- Ask for advice or feedback when needed

- Avoid "all-or-none" thinking—it helps to be flexible

- Let your creativity flow

- Remember that quality of life for you and your family and friends is the ultimate goal

- Assess your QOL progress regularly and adjust goals as needed

## Medical Care Goals

Quality of life can be closely tied to the quality of medical care received. Encourage the client to have the goal of seeking out and obtaining high-quality medical care in which the patient is treated as a collaborative partner. Unfortunately, insurance coverage issues or place of residence might severely limit the available choices. Explore with clients how they will evaluate the quality of their medical care and what they will or can do if that care seems substandard. What is it the client wants or needs from her provider? Emphasize that although evaluating the quality of biomedical interventions may be difficult or impossible for a non-medical person, the client can still evaluate the interpersonal aspects of care and whether her treatment preferences have been respected. If there is an interpersonal problem or conflict with medical providers, review the steps of conflict resolution and the section Getting the Most out of Health Care in Session 8. If there is a symptom management issue affecting QOL, revisit the Symptom Management Worksheet from Session 9.

When the client's disease becomes more advanced, medical care may have to be stepped up. There may come a time when the client is unable to express her wishes. Explain to clients that one way to help ensure that their treatment preferences are met in that time of need is to fill out advanced directives.

## Advanced Directives

Advanced directives are legal documents that are used if one loses the ability to make one's own decisions or express one's wishes. These legal documents are available at most doctors' offices, hospitals, and hospices and can be found online. Clients should be sure to discuss with their doctors which forms need to be filled out. Laws and regulations vary by state and different hospitals may have different procedures or forms.

It is strongly recommended that every person over the age of 18 complete these documents regardless of health status. Stress to the client that it's just a good idea to be prepared to ensure that she will receive the kind of treatment she wants. By having advanced directives the client can still have some control and power even when ill or disabled.

Advanced directives can include a living will and durable power of attorney for health care.

### Living Will

This document specifies what types of medical treatments and death-delaying measures a person wants if she becomes very ill. It includes things like the individual's preferences for resuscitation, artificial breathing, tube feeding, what to do if in a coma, etc.

Ask clients to begin considering what kinds of measures they would like taken. Further explain that a living will is totally unrelated to a regular will, which specifies inheritances, etc. Clients may hear their doctors or medical staff referring to "DNR's" or "DNI's." A DNR/DNI is a do-not-resuscitate and do-not-intubate order. At the patient's request, this order is placed in the medical chart and instructs medical personnel to allow the patient to die peacefully rather than shocking her heart or running tubes down her windpipe for a breathing machine.

### Durable Power of Attorney for Health Care

This document designates a particular individual to make medical decisions on the client's behalf should she be unable to make those decisions herself. This individual can be a family member, friend, or other person. This document is much broader than a living will and covers many more types of possible care decisions.

## Preparing Advanced Directives

Go over with the client the following steps for preparing advanced directives:

1.  Clients should discuss their options with family, friends, and medical providers. Their doctor can explain medical terms and likely scenarios.

2.  Clients should complete the appropriate forms with special attention to their state of residence. It's not necessary to consult an attorney unless desired. A client's doctor, social worker, or other medical team member can provide the forms and help with completion. One popular form that walks clients through this process is called "The Five Wishes" and is widely available for free online. If clients want further information or more forms, they can contact organizations such as the National Hospice Foundation or www.GrowthHouse.org.

3.  The client should designate an individual if filing a durable power of attorney for health care (or DPOA for health care). Clients don't have to have a living will to complete a DPOA for health care form. Since no one can predict all possible medical situations in a living will, the durable power of attorney might be the best bet if clients only want to fill out one form. The client should talk with family and friends about who might be the best agent to designate. The best individual is the one who will be able to carry out the client's wishes—i.e., sometimes the person closest to the client is not the best choice.

4. The client should distribute her directives and keep them nearby. Doctors, medical clinics, family members, etc. should all have copies. In addition, several copies should be kept in accessible locations around the home (e.g., on the refrigerator, by the bed).

5. Clients should periodically review and update their directives. Since circumstances, people, and preferences change, it's a good idea to occasionally review the advanced directives and make any necessary changes. Clients should make sure to inform all involved parties of any changes made.

## End-of-Life or Legacy Projects

Although there is a lot of "business" to take care of in the management of serious disease, there are a number of other less onerous tasks that will assist clients in improving their QOL and processing the emotional demands of this life stage. Refer clients back to their subjective definitions for QOL and the initial goals they have listed to maintain or improve their QOL. Have them consider adding a legacy project to their list of QOL goals. An end-of-life or legacy project is meant to improve the social, psychological, and spiritual aspects of quality of life. (Of course, many of these projects can be beneficial at any life stage.) Examples of creative projects are described as follows.

## Creating a Video Diary

Clients videotape themselves and/or family and friends telling stories, sharing feelings, etc. The videotape may become a treasured gift of recorded history for the next generation. It may also initiate important conversations with loved ones about past events, current feelings, and reasons for gratitude. Variations might include audiotapes or CDs of favorite music, singing, or storytelling.

## Creating a Work of Art

Sometimes, nonverbal expressions of feelings such as paintings, drawings, or sculptures can have powerful impacts on emotional well-being. Artistic talent is irrelevant. The art does not have to be shared and materials can be as simple as paper and crayon. Sometimes a shared art project can be an important bonding experience with family or friends.

## Writing a Letter

People often don't take the time to express their feelings in writing. Have the client think about someone who has been important in her life or about someone or something for which she is grateful. The client can write a "fan letter" or a letter expressing her gratitude and admiration. The letter may have a mood-elevating effect on both the writer and the receiver (Seligman et al., 2005). The client may even consider writing letters without sending them or writing letters to people who can no longer be reached.

## Preparing for the End of the Program

Remind the client that there is only one session remaining in this program. The last session will focus on spirituality and "looking ahead," but the session has been left intentionally unpacked to allow time for clients to bring in their own agenda items. The client should review the entire workbook over the next week and jot down any questions, requests, or observations. Remind clients that this "ending" (i.e., completion of the program) may provide them with an opportunity to practice mood management, coping, communication, and problem solving.

## Homework

✎ Have client finish My Quality of Life (QOL) Worksheet.

✎ Have client finish Goals of the Day form.

✎ Have client finish My Quality of Life Goals form.

✎ Have client consider doing a legacy project.

✎ Have client review the entire workbook and prepare for the last session.

## FAQs from Clients

1. All this talk about quality, pleasure, and enjoyment makes me a little uncomfortable. Life is about hard work, struggle, and keeping a stiff upper lip. Isn't this a little self-absorbed or shallow?

   *A: Life does include work, struggle, and sometimes needing to keep a stiff upper lip. However, it also includes relationships, pleasure, and meaning. This program urges balance and a thoughtful, mindful approach to the decisions we make every day. Time is precious, as is every life. We should carefully choose how we spend it and who we spend it with. That might sometimes mean self-sacrifice, but it might sometimes mean celebrating. Everyone has a right to experience the entirety of life—the good and the bad.*

2. I already feel exhausted and stretched to my limit. How can I set all these new goals and expect to get anything done. It'll just be another disappointment.

   *A: It sounds like a first goal could be to get you some assistance. You do not have to do it all alone. If you are exhausted, let's find someone with the energy to help out. Your goals don't have to be more work. In fact, one goal could be to get more rest.*

3. I can't believe we're already near the end of this program. I need more time. I need more practice. Can't we add on more sessions?

   *A: I find it hard to believe that we are near the end too. You've worked really hard and I am impressed with how much you have accomplished. We will spend part of our last session talking about what to do after the program ends. We can base that plan on how well you are doing now compared with how you were doing when you did the intake assessment. If we find that there are still big issues that need more attention, we will come up with a plan to give you the support you need. Although everyone feels nervous about graduation, most people choose to try these new skills on their own for a while. We can schedule a booster session a few months out or you can always call me if you need to.*

# Session 11 *Resilience, Transcendence, and Spirituality*

*(Corresponds to session 11 of the workbook)*

## Materials Needed

- Flip chart or board
- My Action Plan form

## Outline

- Set agenda
- Review homework
- Introduce resilience and transcendence
- Discuss the importance of spirituality and personal growth
- Discuss open agenda item
- Give program recap and summary
- Elicit client feedback
- Help client plan next steps
- Recommend readings and other resources
- Wrap up program and say goodbye

## Setting the Agenda

Set the agenda by referring to the session outline. Add any topics relevant to the client. Clients should have one or more agenda items to add to this last session. Give the client more control and independence over session management. Encourage them to take the lead with the homework review.

## Homework Review

Review the homework from the last session (QOL definition, measurement, and goals). Have the client identify any obstacles to completing homework and problem solve on his own with you observing and advising as needed. Encourage the client to note his successes over the past week. After this last session, the client will need to reinforce himself on his own and be fully self-motivated.

## Resilience and Transcendence

Given their medical illnesses, many clients may not feel particularly resilient. They may often feel tired, in pain, or just overwhelmed with the daily tasks of coping. Begin the discussion of resilience and transcendence by first providing some introductory definitions, pointing out direct relevance to the client, then illustrating with an inspirational story of a resilient individual (e.g., Victor Frankl, Maya Angelou, Christopher Reeves, Oprah Winfrey, Lance Armstrong, Steven Hawking).

*Resilience* is roughly defined as the capacity to succeed despite the odds. It is the ability to bounce back despite substantial injury. Resilient individuals have often endured great hardship but have managed to pick themselves up, dust themselves off, and continue forward on their journey (often with the help of friends, family, or sometimes strangers). Transcendence takes resilience one step further: not only does the individual survive the hardship, but they are able to learn and grow from that hardship in a way that makes them a better or stronger person. Stories abound of individuals who have grown from injuries or disabilities, or even from learning they are terminally ill. They may no longer be "able-bodied" in the traditional sense but they have become "able-hearted" or "able-spirited"—an accomplishment far more valuable than mere physical functioning.

## Way to Promote Resilience

Given the illness the client is facing, there is most likely a need for resilience and an opportunity for transcendence. Fortunately, there are ways that resilience can be promoted. Ask the client for ideas on ways to help him be more resilient. What has helped in the past? What is realistic in the future?

The following suggestions are taken from the resilience literature and clinical experience (Higgins, 1994; Perkins & Jones, 2004).

*Find a place of refuge or sanctuary.* Everyone needs a "space" to get away from the stressor(s) that is challenging his ability to cope. That place might be a physical location such as a garden, beach, church, or friend's house. It might also be a mental space where the client can go to find rest and relaxation—e.g., meditation, guided imagery, etc.

*Embrace impermanence.* Clients should be reminded that all things come to an end. Good things end, but so do bad things. Pain does not last forever, nor does suffering. The client can probably recall very good and very bad times in his life. In the midst of those times, change might have seemed impossible. But the situation did change. Things always change, even if we can't see how at the moment.

*Believe in control.* Although some things are out of our control, we often have more influence than we believe we have, even if it only means controlling our mood and not the situation. We can manage how we think about a situation. We can control whom we do or don't talk to about the situation. We can control how we choose to cope with an unchangeable situation. Emphasize to clients that regardless of what comes our way, we always have some element of control.

*Draw on the power of relationships.* It is difficult to bear life alone, but with support, we can bear almost anything. Support can come from family, friends, pets, or our sense of spirituality. Remind clients not to be a "lone ranger." Encourage them to ask for help and accept it gratefully.

*Find the "why."* Suffering without a sense of meaning or purpose is perhaps the worst suffering of all. Advise clients to search for the reason why they should pick themselves up and continue forward. What keeps them going? The "silver lining" of their chronic illness might be the opportunity to grow close to loved ones and carefully prepare for handing things off to the next generation. (*Man's Search for Meaning* by Victor Frankl provides a very poignant and in-depth look at how to find meaning in even the most dire of circumstances.)

*Find a role model.* It is hard to know how to move forward if we have never seen anyone do it before. Support groups are a good way to see how others are coping. Inspirational stories and biographies are another good way to see how others have coped or transcended adversity (see suggested reading list at the end of this session).

*Use a "perspective meter."* Suffering is relative to the individual. It arises from the perception of what we have lost. We may be so engrossed in our losses that we forget to look at the bigger picture. Ask clients what gains are still in their lives and what gains might be around the corner. If they look at the sum total of their lives, what are things they can still savor?

*Don't take it personally.* Remind the client that everyone gets sick and everyone dies. If we are lucky, we get some advanced warning and are able to prepare for our deaths. The client has been given the opportunity of appreciating his last days instead of having them end abruptly (as in a sudden accidental death). Stress that the client has every right to feel a wide range of emotions, but what is happening isn't a personal attack on him. What is happening isn't a cosmic injustice or crime. It is sad and it is difficult but it is a natural part of being alive. Encourage the client to let others share this important time with him. It is his time to be center stage.

You may want to use the following dialogue in your discussion:

> *We often think of birth or the first few years of life as being very special and full of wonder. We're right. However, the end of life can be just as special and spiritually meaningful. It's a time to resolve old*

*conflicts, a time to make peace with yourself and your environment, a time to fully realize what's important and what isn't. Being sick often brings things into focus. Although we all must die, being sick makes our mortality seem more real and our life more precious. An ending seems like it may be within sight. As one patient said, "If you go to a play but don't know when it ends, would you pay attention? I think I see the ending and I'm glued to the stage."*

## Spirituality and Personal Growth

Many see spirituality as an important tool for growth and transcendence. Serious illness often activates questions of spirituality regarding ultimate meaning, purpose, and even beliefs about what happens after we die. Spirituality, however, doesn't necessarily refer to a particular religion or set of beliefs. In the broadest sense, it refers to thinking about issues larger than us—i.e., issues about meaning, connection, purpose, and value. It's up to each client to decide if spirituality is important and, if so, what form that spirituality might take.

The following questions are meant to guide and provoke thought. Stress that there are no "right" answers, but an open discussion can help initiate the process of finding the answers that fit for each client. Although it may initially seem odd to discuss issues of spirituality in a medical or "scientific" setting, most clients are eager to discuss these matters. The goal isn't to proselytize or endorse any form of spiritual practice, but rather to support the coping and growth of clients in whatever way they choose.

## Questions for a Psychospiritual Assessment and Exploration

- Is spirituality important to you or your family?

- What are your spiritual beliefs?

- What are your spiritual practices?

- Do you have a spiritual counselor, priest, or clergy? Where do you go for spiritual guidance?

- What gives you a sense of strength or meaning?

- What effect will your illness have on your spiritual practices or beliefs?

- How will your spiritual practices affect your health or health behaviors?

- What are some of the larger questions you've been thinking about since you became ill?

- What do you think happens after you die? Is there anything you need to do to prepare for that?

- How can others help you maintain your source of spiritual strength and meaning during this illness?

## Spiritual Growth Items

Encourage clients to include some spiritual growth items on their lists of short- and long-term goals. Spiritual goals might not change their illness but they can greatly affect the way clients feel. Remind them that spirituality does not necessarily mean religion. Spirituality can include communion with nature, appreciation for science and mathematics, or whatever larger-than-life system they see as worthy of awe. Spiritual practices can include prayer, meditation, music, communion, fellowship, being in nature, etc. Although spirituality can be practiced alone (as with prayer or meditation), remind clients of the importance of social support. Sometimes belonging to a spiritual community (i.e., "finding your tribe") can accomplish the goals of both spiritual and social connections and may even improve physical and mental health (Seybold & Hill, 2001).

## Open Agenda Item

Clients should be encouraged to add an agenda item to this final session. The item could be revisiting a past session where questions still remain, a past homework assignment, new thoughts about how they will cope with their illness, etc. Clients often have questions for their facilitators or anxieties about ending the program. Clients should be reassured that there will still be a recap of the program and a concrete action plan before this final session ends. If the client does not have an agenda item, the recap can sometimes stimulate questions and highlight areas that need to be explained further.

## Recap and Summary

The goal of the recap and summary is to review all of the topics, concepts, and skills covered over the program and to identify any areas still in need of further practice. Take out a blank piece of paper (or go to the white board) and ask the client to list all of the sessions that he remembers and what was learned in each. You should organize these in chronological order even if they are not recalled in that way. Use examples of exercises or stories to prompt the recall of additional sessions.

In short, the organization of the program was as follows:

*Sessions 1–3: Stress and Coping*—stress, breathing, cognition and habits of mind, appraisals, ways of coping, problem solving, A-B-C-D exercise

*Sessions 4–6: Mood Management (Depression, Anxiety, Anger)*—activity scheduling, relaxation, acceptance, forgiveness

*Sessions 7–8: Social Supports*—types of support, support networks, communication, listening, assertiveness, conflict resolution, negotiation

*Sessions 9–11: Quality of Life*—symptom management, end-of-life tasks, goal setting, legacy projects, spirituality, looking forward

Given the breadth and duration of this program, clients are not expected to become experts in any of the skills presented. The introduction to this important skill set, however, should identify fruitful areas where clients can work for greater mastery. The following sections on client feedback and action planning provide a framework for setting these important next steps.

After the summary of the program has been finished, use the list of sessions and skills as a visual aid when asking for specific feedback. Client feedback will be important for developing the client's action plan but also for improving future iterations of the program and honing your skills as a facilitator. Since many have been taught to only provide negative feedback, specific prompts for positive feedback should be included. Start with fairly open-ended questions, then narrow the focus as needed. For example:

- *What is the single most important, memorable, or useful thing you learned from this program?*

- *How will your participation in this program continue to affect you once we finish today?*

- *Are there any concepts, ideas, or other areas of importance that we didn't cover or maybe didn't spend enough time on?*

- *If you could do this program all over again, what would you change about it? What would you do differently? What should your facilitator do differently?*

## Planning Next Steps—Action Plan

If appropriate, additional visits can be scheduled. Some clients find it helpful to have at least one booster session scheduled in the not too distant future. Although this may be seen as encouraging dependence in traditional therapy models, clients at the end of life are in need of support and not "sink-or-swim" interventions to promote independence. Preliminary research in CBT for depression also suggests that booster sessions may be helpful (Clarke et al., 1999). In general, perhaps treatment for mental illness and distress should be conceptually broadened to include ongoing mental health promotion and prevention with occasional "check-ups" as needed—i.e., achieving and keeping mental health is a lifelong process.

Have clients turn to the Action Plan in the workbook. Clients should reflect on the program recap and feedback they have just provided. Clients should also recall the goals set in Sessions 1 and 10. While those goals focused more on ways to improve quality of life, the Action Plan is intended to outline a course of self-study to assist the client in using and deepening newly acquired skills. Many clients find it helpful to schedule ongoing "appointments" with themselves or times set aside to specifically work on the skills in their workbook. (You may suggest clients do this at the same time your weekly sessions used to take place.)

Over the past 10 sessions, clients have amassed a collection of strategies to identify, monitor, and manage stress, mood, relationships, and medical symptoms. Clients will naturally resonate with some strategies but not others. Clients may want to list their favorite strategies as part of their Action Plan. The following short list is intended to provide a few additional ideas for how clients may work to better improve their quality of life.

### Keeping a Journal: Variations on a Theme

It is a long-held belief that expressive writing such as keeping a diary or journal can promote health. The research of James Pennebaker and others is starting to corroborate this claim (Broderick, Junghaenel, & Schwartz, 2005; Petrie, Fontanilla, Thomas, Booth, & Pennebaker, 2004). Although the precise mechanisms of action are unknown, journaling may provide a catharsis, speed emotional processing, and "contain" worries or other problems on paper in place of rumination, etc. The precise "dose" required is also unknown and the effective format appears to be flexible (i.e., the journal can be written, electronic, etc.). In most research studies, subjects are given prompts to encourage them to write about an emotionally charged event for 15–20 minutes—e.g., write about an event that really upset them, detail what happened, why they think it happened, how it affects their life, etc. Specific instructions and variations can be found in Pennebaker's layperson book, *Writing to Heal* (2004).

Although not empirically supported, clients may want a more focused and mood-uplifting journal format that influences selective attention and promotes savoring. At the end of each day, clients are encouraged to take about 10–15 minutes to answer three questions:

- What surprised me today?

- What moved me today?

- What inspired me today?

If time permits, ask the clients to complete this exercise during the session (see workbook). They may note an immediate mood impact. Encourage them to test out this mood effect over time by answering these three questions every night for several weeks. An empirically supported variant of this exercise asks clients to recall three things that went well today, then provide a causal explanation for each positive event (Seligman et al., 2005). Clients can use their new self-monitoring skills to assess the impact.

Another variant combines journaling with creating an end-of-life legacy project. Clients combine journal entries (written or electronic) with poetry, artwork, old photos, or MP3s of favorite songs, etc. The journal can be a collaborative effort with loved ones or be passed on as a gift for others to enjoy. The goal is to be creative and expressive while savoring positive memories and improving mood.

## Letters to the Medical Team

The idea of gratitude or "fan letters" was presented in Session 10. As mentioned earlier, these letters can be shared or they can be saved as a collection of memoirs. Since most clients will have many interactions with medical staff, encourage them to express their appreciation when someone does something good or kind. For some clients, their doctor or hospice worker will become like a member of the family. Ask clients to consider whether they would like to write a letter to any medical professionals in their lives. Remind them that letters do not have to be given to the person.

## Recommended Readings and Other Resources for Clients

First-person narratives, self-help, and other inspirational books can be important tools for a client's action plan. This guide and the client workbook both include an appendix with a very brief list of books that clients may enjoy. The Appendix also includes information on helpful Web sites and organizations.

## Program Wrap-up and Saying Goodbye

The ending of treatment should be conceptualized as an important opportunity to practice saying goodbye. With their new skills in self-monitoring, cognition, and communication, clients should have some grasp of what they are feeling, why they are feeling it, and how to communicate it in the moment. Facilitators can model direct expressions of feelings, acknowledgment of the ending, and savoring of a shared moment of tender intimacy. Any plans for future booster sessions or referrals to more in-depth treatment programs, support groups, etc. should be settled before the client leaves. Depending on client preference and need, significant others may be invited to the last session to learn about and shape the post-termination plan.

# Program Adaptations

## Program Intention and Flexibility

The Minding the Body program was originally developed as a structured therapy group for patients with congestive heart failure, COPD, and cancer. Significant others, family, or caregivers were invited to attend and participate as were all of the staff members of the Comprehensive Care Team (i.e., doctors, social workers, nurses, chaplain, and trainees). Although participants were encouraged to complete the full program, it was recognized that attendance might be more sporadic or difficult to predict given the substantial medical burden faced by some of the participants. As a consequence, several treatment variations were developed to respond to the clients' changing needs. Since its inception, Minding the Body has evolved into an outpatient, individual therapy program that sometimes includes phone appointments and special sessions that take place on the inpatient unit when the patient is hospitalized. However, depending on facilitator preferences, resources, and client needs, the program can still be run as a group (as originally intended) or otherwise adapted. Important group issues are discussed in this chapter, as are special considerations for telephone sessions, home visits, and couples or family formats.

## Group Meetings and Program Duration

Minding the Body was initially developed as a group treatment. The original program included twelve 90-minute sessions that met once per week in an ambulatory care setting. The group was organized into two six-session "modules" with the first module starting with stress (the current Session 1 in the individual version) and ending with anger management (the current Session 6). The second module started with a repeat of the introductory stress session and continued to the end of the current program (i.e., social supports, communication, symptom management, goal setting, spirituality). This modular format was developed to allow new members to enter the group every 6 weeks instead of having to wait for up to 12 weeks for a new cohort to begin. At any given time, there could be both junior (i.e., starting their first module) and senior (i.e., starting their second module) members in the group. This mixed composition and rapid turnover could negatively affect cohesion, but it also had the unforeseen advantage of giving senior members the opportunity to teach junior members. Senior members could be quite effective in "selling" the group, passing down a constructive group culture, and modeling effective coping behaviors.

## Group Size and Composition

Although a group is more than the sum of its parts, careful attention to group size and composition are essential to healthy group process and outcome. The optimal size of a group is usually defined as 6–12 members, giving the group enough critical mass but not overwhelming in size. Given the emotional intensity of the issues that clients may be facing, smaller group sizes are preferred. Ultimately the composition and size will depend on facilitator ability and the extent of any unique needs of particular group members.

Greater member homogeneity (i.e., along the lines of gender, diagnosis, age, etc.) is usually related to more rapid cohesion, immediate provision of support, better attendance, and more rapid symptom relief. However, homogenous groups are more likely to remain at superficial levels of interaction and are thought to be less effective in producing more fundamental interpersonal learning. There is currently a need for research to explore the tradeoff between interpersonal learning (heterogeneity) and ensuring group maintenance (homogeneity). A meta-analysis of the composition literature concludes that highly structured groups may suppress composition effects (Waltman & Zimpfer, 1988). In contrast, Salvendy (1993) argues that short-term groups should be homogenous in regard to diagnosis and level of stress tolerance because of the necessity to bond and work quickly. Ultimately, any collection of individuals in a group may need to be guided in the process of identifying and bonding with one another in order to best utilize curative group factors.

## Screening and Pre-Group Training

All clients being considered for the group should be screened as in the individual protocol. Interpersonal style and presence of Axis II pathology should receive special attention before addition to any group. Most clients will express a preference for treatment in an individual format, citing worries about privacy, social anxiety, and/or fears of becoming more "depressed" from hearing the stories of others. If an individual format is not available or the client might greatly benefit from group curative factors, the client should be reminded that individual therapy is not more efficacious and lacks both the wisdom and support that comes from a group of other clients who "know what its like." While individual therapy does provide more freedom to individualize the focus of each session, it misses the substantial benefit of the group curative factors discussed below.

Patients typically do not possess important group skills and hold negative expectations about group experiences. In response, group therapists have relied on pre-group training programs and have established basic group rules and guidelines. Multiple methods of training, particularly those that are interactive (video tapes, practice sessions, etc.), are most effective (Kivlighan, Corazinni, & McGovern, 1985). Training procedures usually consist of individual sessions (lasting 15–45 minutes) emphasizing the safe and supportive qualities of a group, basic education about group roles and process, the benefits of self-disclosure, interpersonal feedback, here-and-now interactions, therapeutic factors, and realistic prognostic expectations. Members are also given a solid rationale for group treatment emphasizing the interpersonal nature of the presenting complaint. Research on pre-group training has demonstrated the advantages and effectiveness of pre-training strategies, particularly in the alleviation of anxiety, reduction of premature attrition, and improved outcome reports (Beutler, Crago, & Arizmendi, 1986; Piper & Perrault, 1989).

Coping with end-of-life issues is an ongoing process. This program is intended to provide important skills that will help the client and her family navigate the challenging issues that might emerge as her illness progresses. Although a client may show substantial improvement upon graduation, new stressors may occur requiring additional visits. In order to capture emerging problems and to best reinforce and elaborate the skills taught in this program, booster sessions or, in the case of groups, "class reunions" are recommended at 3, 6, and 12 months after program completion. Alternatively, phone or e-mail check-ins can be used. Each booster session or contact should include a brief assessment of mood, functioning, and quality of life to identify possible areas of focus. Past groups have also started their own unmoderated electronic discussion boards to stay connected and continue to provide support. Regardless of the avenue chosen, clients should be reminded to reassess themselves regularly and use the skills taught in this program.

## Role of Group Facilitators

Group facilitators are actively engaged in this hands-on, skill-based program. The level of activity and engagement is similar to that of individual cognitive-behavioral therapy (CBT), where agendas are collaboratively set and problem solving is actively used for whatever issues might arise. In a group, there is less freedom for individualizing sessions; however, there are more opportunities for client–client interactions and other group curative factors. The term *facilitator* is used rather than *leader* to reflect the philosophy of client and group-centered learning. The facilitator provides structure and expertise while directing client and group energies in productive directions. Although the facilitator is an active agent of change, the primary power resides within the client and her peers.

Given the range and intensity of issues that may be covered in the group, a co-facilitation model can be helpful particularly when co-facilitators come from different disciplines (e.g., nursing and psychology). In training centers, a senior–junior facilitator pair can provide an important teaching opportunity while increasing the personal attention the client and the group receive. The responsibilities and level of involvement for each facilitator will vary by level of experience and ability.

## Training Group Facilitators

The Minding the Body group program was originally developed and led by a clinical psychologist with occasional co-facilitation by a nurse, social worker, chaplain, and a palliative care physician depending on session content. Although ideal, this range of expertise is not necessary. The group may be facilitated by one individual who has sufficient experience with cognitive-behavioral interventions and group therapy. Master's level counselors, social workers, nurse practitioners, or others may qualify.

The basic philosophy of this program supports the hospice model of multidisciplinary end-of-life care but brings mental health and other psychosocial concerns to the foreground. If multidisciplinary co-facilitators cannot be used, it is hoped that multidisciplinary consultations will occur outside of the group context. It is recommended that all group facilitators of any level have regular consultations and support depending on their level of competence and the level of difficulty the group presents.

For trainees, the ideal model is one of senior–junior co-facilitation. If co-facilitation cannot be used, supervision can be provided using videotaped sessions. Treatment quality and adherence can be monitored and assessed using the Cognitive Therapy Scale (Vallis, Shaw, & Dobson, 1980) for general CBT therapeutic skills and following a treatment outline for specific protocol fidelity. This guide also includes an appendix with fidelity checklists providing outlines of each session. Facilitators may find it helpful to record time estimates for each session element. You may photocopy forms from the book as needed.

## Curative Factors and Group Process

Although Minding the Body is a structured, time-limited program strongly based in cognitive-behavioral therapy, the group version should not simply be a class of individuals simultaneously receiving individual therapy. Therapy should be *through* the group rather than simply *in* the group. A number of group curative factors should be employed to deepen interpersonal learning and actively practice new skills in the "here-and-now." Classic group curative factors include the instillation of hope, universality, imparting of information, altruism, corrective recapitulation of the primary family group, development of socializing techniques, imitative behavior, interpersonal learning, group cohesiveness, catharsis, and existential factors (Yalom, 1985). While some factors such as group cohesion and imitative behaviors (i.e., modeling) have received empirical support, others remain more theoretical.

At minimum, group therapy can be conceptualized as exposing individuals to multiple peer models and encouraging observational learning. Clients with mild to moderate levels of distress or those who rapidly respond to therapy can serve as mastery and coping models for the slower or more seriously disturbed clients. The group audience also increases the likelihood for social reinforcement that could enhance individual motivation and encourage pro-therapeutic change. In a cohesive group, adherence to homework assignments, regular attendance, and participation are improved due to their increased value as rewards (Satterfield, 1994). Though reinforcement can and does occur in individual settings, a group setting can significantly increase both the frequency and intensity of personal rewards.

It is helpful to think of a group as a dynamic, complex system that progresses through stages from its "birth" to its "termination." Common group processes such as identity formation, setting of group norms, establishment of basic trust, and group cohesion affect the health of the group and its overall level of effectiveness. Group processes are heavily dependent on group structure and composition but also grow from shared group experiences facilitated by the group leader. An understanding of group developmental milestones, group cohesion, levels of interventions, and therapeutic factors can lay the foundation for successful group facilitation. For further discussion of classic group process variables see Rutan & Stone (2000), Yalom (1985), or Kaplan & Sadock (1993).

In the initial phase of group development, orientation, acceptance, fear of rejection, ambivalence, and dependency on the leader(s) are central issues. The second phase is usually labeled as the differentiation, rebellion, early working phase, or "prelude-to-crisis" stage. Here, members are more comfortable in the group and begin to clearly exhibit their interpersonal habits and symptoms. The remaining stages usually involve a stabilization of the group through which a great deal of therapeutic work can occur along with the more traditional personal growth associated with psychodynamic therapy. The final stage, termination, activates issues of abandonment, loss, regression, and evaluation—issues that are of critical importance for clients near the end of life.

Basic CBT structure meshes well with group dynamics by facilitating cohesion and the stage-like progression of a group. Literature reviews show that over 80% of the studies comparing structured CBT group techniques with more ambiguous interventions found structured groups to be superior in outcome and process measures (Dies, 1993). The structure reduces the ambiguity of the therapeutic task, alleviates initial anxiety, teaches important group and cognitive skills, clarifies expectations, and increases risk taking and cohesion building (Satterfield, 1994).

## Troubleshooting

In addition to the challenges faced in an individual format, a group approach may raise special concerns around client–client conflict, confidentiality, attendance, and other adherence issues. It should be remembered that the power in a group format lies within the group—i.e., problems can often be discussed and solved by the group rather than handled solely by the facilitator. A clear discussion of group norms (e.g., respect, confidentiality, attendance) should be done in the first session and revisited if needed. Special dyadic sessions can be scheduled if interpersonal conflicts arise that cannot be settled by the group. Consultation from other professionals outside the group can often be helpful in resolving these and other difficult group dynamics issues.

Attendance and other adherence issues may be handled differently in this client population. Given the medical burden faced by the participants, attendance or homework completion may not be as regular as desired. The reasons for non-adherence should be carefully explored with the understanding that although non-adherence can have psychodynamic significance, it may also be due to uncontrollable and excusable factors.

Examples of flexible adaptations include allowing the client to participate in the group by speaker phone, facilitator and/or group members calling the absent client in between visits, or offering an individual make-up session. Non-adherence to homework can be used as a here-and-now demonstration of problem-solving skills in which all group members can participate and learn.

## Telephone and Internet Sessions

Current research is exploring the use of various forms of technology as delivery vehicles for CBT. For clients with impaired mobility or limited transportation or those living in a rural area, CBT can be delivered by telephone or Internet. Telephone CBT (T-CBT) has been successfully used for the treatment of depression in clients with multiple sclerosis and as a more supportive tool for clients with breast cancer (Mohr et al., 2005; Sandgren & McCaul, 2007). Online Web sites and e-mail communication offer the same convenience with the added possibility of visual and written materials but perhaps with less emotional connection. Although open Web sites suffer from high attrition and poor outcomes, systematic reviews and meta-analyses have shown that direct e-mails from therapist-monitored sites can successfully be used to treat depression and anxiety (Christensen, Griffiths, Mackinnon, & Brittliffe, 2006; Kaltenthaler et al., 2006; Spek et al., 2007). Almost no research has looked at the delivery of CBT in home visits with the exception of a promising program to treat postpartum depression (Chabrol et al., 2002).

For this program, clients may use telephone and e-mail contact to make up sessions missed due to medical or other reasons. If possible, facilitators may utilize home or hospital visits. At this time, these delivery vehicles are seen as supplements to more standard individual or group formats. However, if appropriate assessments can be made and a therapeutic alliance established, facilitators may opt for larger segments delivered in these formats. Special issues around competence, ethics, and other necessary style modifications should be explored first before pursuing these innovative but mostly untested formats.

Many of the issues germane to clients at the beginning of the end of life are interpersonal in nature. Friends, families, and caregivers are often eager to provide care but require guidance and support. Clients may request that significant individuals attend some or all sessions of this program. In its original group format, caregivers were welcome to join the group but were expected to participate as any client. It was assumed that most caregivers could also benefit from stress reduction and mood management interventions. The presence of caregivers for Session 7 (Social Supports) and Session 8 (Communication and Conflict Resolution) should receive special consideration. While these two sessions are most closely relevant to the interpersonal issues the client may be facing, having a caregiver present might interfere with a client's ability to be open and honest. If overt conflict exists in the dyad or family, these sessions are likely to activate those issues and may be quite difficult to manage in a group setting. On the other hand, the here-and-now demonstration of these conflicts with both parties present might provide an unprecedented opportunity for assisted communication and resolution.

Caregivers might also have a specific interest in Session 9 (Symptom Management). Caregivers often feel unprepared to respond to the exacerbation of a client's symptoms and appreciate specific and concrete advice. Although Session 9 can serve as a useful introduction to symptom management, caregivers are encouraged to follow up this introduction with a more in-depth caregiver course such as those offered by the American Cancer Society or local hospices. As a client advances toward the later stages of the end of life, caregivers take on larger and larger roles that may include medical decision making and administration of medication or other medical interventions. While beyond the scope of this program, interested providers can be directed to other resources to address these needs (e.g., McFarlane & Bashe, 1998; Rabow, Hauser, & Adams, 2004).

Special training and preparation is required for facilitators who choose a couples or family therapy format. These formats may present very complex and difficult family dynamics with decades of suppressed resentments and maladaptive communication. Helpful treatment guidelines for these formats can be found in Bowen (2002), Minuchin (1977), and Coche' & Satterfield (1993). It should be assumed that families will become more involved in the client's care at some point in the future regardless of what treatment format is chosen. Ideally, this will occur before an inpatient family conference regarding final care decisions.

# Appendix    *Bibliotherapy and Clinical Resources*

## Inspiration and Spirituality

Bolen, J. (2007). *Close to the bone: Life-threatening illness as a soul journey* (10th Anv. Rev. ed.). San Francisco: Conari Press.

Canfield, J., & Hansen, M. V. (1992). *Chicken soup for the soul: 101 stories to open the heart and rekindle the spirit.* Deerfield Beach, FL: Health Communications.

Chodron, P. (2000). *When things fall apart: Heart advice for difficult times* (New ed.). Boston: Shambhala Publications.

Frankl, V. (2006). *Man's search for meaning.* Boston: Beacon Press.

Kabat-Zinn, J. (2005). *Wherever you go, there you are: mindfulness meditation in everyday life* (10th Anv. ed.) New York: Hyperion.

Remen, R. (2006). *Kitchen table wisdom: Stories that heal* (10th Anv. ed.). New York: Riverhead Books.

Salzberg, S. (2002). *Loving-kindness: The revolutionary art of happiness* (Rev. ed.). Boston, MA: Shambhala Publications.

Siegel, B. (1990). *Love, medicine, and miracles: Lessons learned about self-healing from a surgeon's experience with exceptional patients.* New York: Harper Paperbacks.

Siegel, B. (2003). *365 prescriptions for the soul: Daily messages of inspiration, hope, and love.* Novato, CA: New World Library.

## Mood and Stress Management

Burns, D. (1999). *Feeling good: The new mood therapy* (Rev. ed.). New York: Avon.

Davis, M., Eshelman, E., & McKay, M. (2000). *The relaxation and stress reduction workbook* (5th ed.). Oakland, CA: New Harbinger Publications.

Greenberger, D., & Padesky, C. (1995). *Mind over mood: Change how you feel by changing the way you think.* New York: Guilford Press.

Hayes, S. (2005). *Get out of your mind and into your life: The new acceptance and commitment therapy.* Oakland, CA: New Harbinger Publications.

McKay, M., Davis, M., & Fanning, P. (2007). *Thoughts and feelings: Taking control of your moods and your life* (3rd ed.). Oakland, CA: New Harbinger Publications.

Pennebaker, J. W. (2004) *Writing to heal: A guided journal for recovering from trauma and emotional upheaval.* Oakland, CA: New Harbinger Publications.

Seligman, M. (1998). *Learned optimism: How to change your mind and your life.* New York: Free Press.

Seligman, M. (2002). *Authentic happiness: Using the new positive psychology to realize your potential for lasting fulfillment.* New York: Free Press.

### Anxiety and Panic

Bourne, E. (2005). *The anxiety and phobia workbook* (4th ed). Oakland, CA: New Harbinger Publications.

Willliams, M. B., & Poijula, S. (2002). *The PTSD workbook: Simple, effective techniques for overcoming traumatic stress symptoms.* Oakland, CA: New Harbinger Publications.

Zuercher-White, E. (1998). *An end to panic: Breakthrough techniques for overcoming panic disorder* (2nd ed.). Oakland, CA: New Harbinger Publications.

### Anger and Forgiveness

Flanigan, B. (1994). *Forgiving the unforgivable: Overcoming the bitter legacy of intimate wounds.* New York: Wiley.

Luskin, F. (2003). *Forgive for good: A proven prescription for health and happiness.* New York: HarperOne.

McKay, M., Rogers, P., & McKay, J. (1989). *When anger hurts: Quieting the storm within.* Oakland, CA: New Harbinger Publications.

Williams, R., & Williams, V. (1998). *Anger kills: Seventeen strategies for controlling the hostility that can harm your health.* New York: HarperTorch.

### Communication and Conflict Resolution

Fisher, R., Patton, B. M., & Ury, W. L. (1992). *Getting to yes: Negotiating agreement without giving in* (2nd ed.). Boston: Houghton Mifflin.

McKay, M., Davis, M., & Fanning, P. (1995). *Messages: The communication skills* (2nd ed.) Oakland, CA: New Harbinger Publications.

McKay, M., Fanning, P., & Paleg, K. (2006). *Couple skills: Making your relationship work* (2nd Rev ed.). Oakland, CA: New Harbinger Publications.

### End-of-Life Issues

Byock, I. (1997). *Dying well: The prospect for growth at the end of life*. New York: Riverhead Books.

Lynn, J., & Harrold, J. (2001). *Handbook for mortals: Guidance for people facing serious illness* (New ed.). New York: Oxford University Press.

McFarlane, R., & Bashe, P. (1999). *The complete bedside companion: No-nonsense advice on caring for the seriously ill*. New York: Fireside.

Nuland, S. (1995). *How we die: Reflections on life's final chapter*. New York: Vintage.

Olive, B. (1998). *Time to say goodbye: What everyone needs to know*. Milwaukee, WI: LeMieux International Ltd.

### Web sites and Organizations

Aging with Dignity—The Five Wishes
   http://www.agingwithdignity.org/
   Tel: (888) 5WISHES (594–7437)

Americans for Better Care of the Dying
   http://www.abcd-caring.org/
   Tel: 703–647–8505

Caring Connections, National Hospice and Palliative Care Organization
   http://www.caringinfo.org/
   Help Line: 800–658–8898
   Spanish Help Line: 877–658–8896

Growth House, Inc.
   http://www.growthhouse.org
   Tel: 415–863–3045

# Fidelity Checklists

**Session 1: Medical Illness and Stress**

**Fidelity Checklist**

Client Name: _____ Date: _____

Rate your fidelity to each session element on a scale of 1 to 7, with 1 indicating poor fidelity and 7 indicating high fidelity.

_____ Give overview of the program

_____ Introduce the concept of mind-body medicine

_____ Introduce the cycle of medical illness and stress

_____ Discuss stress and its symptoms

_____ Preview stress and coping module

_____ Review assessment results and set initial goals

_____ Conduct breathing exercise

_____ Assign homework

Notes:

_____

_____

_____

_____

_____

## Session 2: Stress, Thinking, and Appraisals

### Fidelity Checklist

Client Name: _____ Date: _____

Rate your fidelity to each session element on a scale of 1 to 7, with 1 indicating poor fidelity and 7 indicating high fidelity.

_____ Set the agenda

_____ Review homework

_____ Review previous session

_____ Introduce the cognitive component of stress management

_____ Present helpful (versus hurtful) ways of thinking

_____ Conduct helpful thoughts exercise

_____ Discuss common habits of mind

_____ Help client start to capture cognitions

_____ Link thinking with stress appraisals

_____ Conduct appraisal exercise

_____ Assign homework

Notes:

_____

_____

_____

_____

_____

## Session 3: Coping with Stress: Problem-Focused and Emotion-Focused Strategies

### Fidelity Checklist

Client Name: _____ Date: _____

Rate your fidelity to each session element on a scale of 1 to 7, with 1 indicating poor fidelity and 7 indicating high fidelity.

_____ Set agenda

_____ Review homework

_____ Use appraisals to guide coping

_____ Discuss problem-focused coping

_____ Discuss emotion-focused coping

_____ Conduct affirmation exercise

_____ Introduce A-B-C-D exercise

_____ Assign homework

Notes:

_____

_____

_____

_____

_____

_____

_____

## Session 4: Illness and Mood: Depression

### Fidelity Checklist

Client Name: _____ Date: _____

Rate your fidelity to each session element on a scale of 1 to 7, with 1 indicating poor fidelity and 7 indicating high fidelity.

_____ Set agenda

_____ Review homework

_____ Define and discuss depression

_____ Discuss medication as a treatment for depression

_____ Discuss therapy as a treatment for depression

_____ Discuss self-help as a treatment for depression

_____ Introduce activity monitoring and scheduling

_____ Introduce Pleasant Activities List

_____ Assign homework

Notes:

_____

_____

_____

_____

_____

_____

## Session 5: Illness and Mood: Anxiety

### Fidelity Checklist

Client Name: _____ Date: _____

Rate your fidelity to each session element on a scale of 1 to 7, with 1 indicating poor fidelity and 7 indicating high fidelity.

_____ Set agenda

_____ Review homework

_____ Define anxiety and review common symptoms

_____ Introduce steps for dealing with anxiety

_____ Discuss self-help as a treatment for anxiety

_____ Conduct diaphragmatic breathing

_____ Conduct progressive muscle relaxation and/or guided imagery

_____ Discuss medication as a treatment for anxiety

_____ Discuss therapy as a treatment for anxiety

_____ Review steps for dealing with anxiety

_____ Assign homework

Notes:

_____

_____

_____

_____

## Session 6: Illness and Mood: Anger

### Fidelity Checklist

Client Name: _____ Date: _____

Rate your fidelity to each session element on a scale of 1 to 7, with 1 indicating poor fidelity and 7 indicating high fidelity.

_____ Set agenda

_____ Review homework

_____ Define anger and discuss common expressions of anger

_____ Discuss how to identify angry feelings

_____ Discuss how to identify the source of anger

_____ Discuss how to problem solve around anger

_____ Discuss how to ease one's mind

_____ Discuss acceptance and forgiveness

_____ Assign homework

Notes:

_____

_____

_____

_____

_____

_____

**Fidelity Checklist**

Client Name: _____ Date: _____

Rate your fidelity to each session element on a scale of 1 to 7, with 1 indicating poor fidelity and 7 indicating high fidelity.

_____ Set agenda

_____ Review homework

_____ Define and review types of support

_____ Help client identify social support network

_____ Help client evaluate social supports

_____ Discuss the steps for expressing support needs

_____ Assign homework

Notes:

_____

_____

_____

_____

_____

_____

_____

_____

## Session 8: Communication and Conflict Resolution

### Fidelity Checklist

Client Name: _____ Date: _____

Rate your fidelity to each session element on a scale of 1 to 7, with 1 indicating poor fidelity and 7 indicating high fidelity.

_____ Set agenda

_____ Review homework

_____ Discuss the importance of good communication

_____ Discuss active listening

_____ Discuss how to express oneself effectively

_____ Present elements of conflict resolution

_____ Discuss the importance of quality time for strong relationships

_____ Give suggestions for getting the most out of health care

_____ Assign homework

Notes:

_____

_____

_____

_____

_____

Client Name: _____ Date: _____

Rate your fidelity to each session element on a scale of 1 to 7, with 1 indicating poor fidelity and 7 indicating high fidelity.

_____ Set agenda

_____ Review homework

_____ Discuss how to manage medical symptoms

_____ Give tips for coping with chronic pain

_____ Give tips for coping with insomnia or sleep problems

_____ Give tips for coping with other common medical symptoms

_____ Close discussion on symptom management

_____ Assign homework

Notes:

_____

_____

_____

_____

_____

_____

## Session 10: Quality of Life: Setting Goals and Looking Forward

### Fidelity Checklist

Client Name: _____ Date: _____

Rate your fidelity to each session element on a scale of 1 to 7, with 1 indicating poor fidelity and 7 indicating high fidelity.

_____ Set agenda

_____ Review homework

_____ Introduce palliative care and hospice

_____ Discuss quality of life (QOL) construct

_____ Help client set QOL goals

_____ Discuss how to achieve goals

_____ Review medical goals including advanced directives

_____ Have the client consider doing an end-of-life or legacy project

_____ Prepare client for upcoming end of the program

Notes:

_____

_____

_____

_____

_____

_____

**Fidelity Checklist**

Client Name: _____ Date: _____

Rate your fidelity to each session element on a scale of 1 to 7, with 1 indicating poor fidelity and 7 indicating high fidelity.

_____ Set agenda

_____ Review homework

_____ Introduce resilience and transcendence

_____ Discuss the importance of spirituality and personal growth

_____ Discuss open agenda item

_____ Give program recap and summary

_____ Elicit client feedback

_____ Help client plan next steps

_____ Recommend readings and other resources

_____ Wrap up program and say goodbye

Notes:

_____

_____

_____

_____

_____

# References

Abbey, J. G., Rosenfeld, B., Pessin, H., & Breitbart, W. (2006). Hopelessness at the end of life: The utility of the hopelessness scale with terminally ill cancer patients. *British Journal of Health Psychology, 11*(2), 173–183.

Adler, N., & Matthews, K. (1994). Health psychology: Why do some people stay sick and some stay well? *Annual Review of Psychology, 45,* 229–259.

American College of Physicians. (1989). *Ethics manual.* Washington, DC: Author.

American Psychiatric Association. (2000). *Diagnostic and statistical manual of mental disorders* (4th ed., text revised). Washington, DC: Author.

American Psychological Association. (2002). Ethical principles of psychologists and code of conduct. *American Psychologist, 57,* 1060–1073.

Anderson, C.A., & Bushman. B.J. (2002). Human aggression. *Annual Review of Psychology, 53,* 27–51.

Antoni, M. H., Lechner, S. C., Kazi, A., Wimberly, S. R., Sifre, T., Urcuyo, K. R., Phillips, K., Gluck, S., & Carver, C. S. (2006). How stress management improves quality of life after treatment for breast cancer. *Journal of Consulting and Clinical Psychology, 74(6),* 1143–1152.

Arean, P. (2001). Group to Learn about Depression (GLAD) Manual. Unpublished manuscript.

Barefoot, J.C., Dodge, K.A., Peterson, B.L., Dahlstrom, W.G., & Williams, R.B. (1989). The Cook-Medley hostility scale: item content and ability to predict survival. *Psychosomatic Medicine, Vol 51,* 46–57.

Beck, A.T., Epstein, N., Brown, G., & Steer R. (1988). An inventory for measuring clinical anxiety. Psychometric properties. Journal of Consulting and Clinical Psychology, *56,* 893–897.

Beck, A. T., Rush, A. J., Shaw, B. F., & Emery, G. (1979). *Cognitive therapy of depression.* New York: Guilford Press.

Beck, A. T., Ward, C. H., Mendelson, M., Mock, J., & Erbaugh, J. (1961). An inventory for measuring depression. *Archives of Internal Medicine, 154,* 2039–2047.

Beck, A. T., Weismann, A., Lester, D., & Trexler, L. (1974). The measurement of pessimism: The Beck Hopelessness Scale. *Journal of Consulting and Clinical Psychology, 42,* 861–865.

Benson, H., & Klipper, M. (2000). *The relaxation response* (Expanded updated ed.). New York: Harper Paperbacks.

Beutler, L.E., Crago, M., & Arizmendi, T.G. (1986). Research on therapist variables in psychotherapy. In S. L. Garfield & A. E. Bergin (Eds.), *Handbook of psychotherapy and behavior change* (2nd ed., pp. 257–310). New York: Wiley.

Bodenheimer, T., Lorig, K., Halstead, H., & Grumbach, K. (2002). Patient self-management of chronic disease in primary care. *Journal of the American Medical Association, 288,* 2469–2475.

Bowen, M. (2002). *Family therapy in clinical practice.* New York: Aronson.

Brady, M., Peterman, A., Fitchett, G., Mo, M., & Cella, D. (1999). A case for including spirituality in quality of life measurement in oncology. *Psychooncology,* 8 , 417–428.

Broadhead, W., Gehlbach, S., De Gruy, F., & Kaplan, B. (1988). The Duke-UNC Functional Social Support Questionnaire: measurement of social support in family medicine patients. *Medical Care,* 26 , 709–723.

Broderick, J. E., Junghaenel, D. U., & Schwartz, J. E. (2005). Written emotional expression produces health benefits in fibromyalgia patients. *Psychosomatic Medicine 67(2),* 326–334.

Burish, T. G., & Jenkins, R. A. (1992). Effectiveness of biofeedback and relaxation training in reducing the side effects of cancer chemotherapy. *Health Psychology 11(1),* 17–23.

Burns, D. (1981). *Feeling good: The new mood therapy.* New York: New American Library.

Byock, I. (1997). *Dying well: The prospect for growth at the end of life.* New York: Riverhead Books.

Byock, I., & Merriman, M. (1998). Measuring quality of life for patients with terminal illness: the Missoula–VITAS(r) quality of life index. *Palliative Medicine, 12,* 231–244.

Carver, C. (1997). You want to Measure Coping But Your Protocol's Too Long: Consider the Brief COPE. *International Journal of Behavioral Medicine, Vol. 4,* 92–100.

Cella, D.F., Jacobson, P.B., Orlav, E.J., & Holland, J.C. (1987). A briefs POMS measure of distress for cancer patients. *Journal of Chronic Diseases, 40,* 939–942.

Chabrol, H., Teissedre, F., Saint-Jean, M., Teisseyre, N., Roge, B., & Mullet, E. (2002). Prevention and treatment of post-partum depression: a controlled randomized study on women at risk. *Psychological Medicine, 32(6)*, 1039–1047.

Chang, B. H., Hendricks, A., Zhao, Y., Rothendler, J. A., LoCastro, J. S., & Slawsky, M. T. (2005). A relaxation response randomized trial on patients with chronic heart failure. *Journal of Cardiopulmonary Rehabilitation*, 25(3), 149–157.

Chesney, M. A., Chambers, D. B., Taylor, J. M., Johnson, L. M., & Folkman, S. (2003). Coping effectiveness training for men living with HIV: Results from a randomized clinical trial testing a group-based intervention. *Psychosomatic Medicine, 65(6)*, 1038–1046.

Christensen, H., Griffiths, K. M., Mackinnon, A. J., & Brittliffe, K. (2006). Online randomized controlled trial of brief and full cognitive behaviour therapy for depression. *Psychological Medicine, 36(12)*, 1737–1746.

Clarke, G. N., Rohde, P., Lewinsohn, P. M., Hops, H., & Seeley, J. R. (1999). Cognitive-behavioral treatment of adolescent depression: Efficacy of acute group treatment and booster sessions. Journal of the American Academy of Child & Adolescent Psychiatry , *38(3)*, 272–279.

Coche,' J. M., & Satterfield, J. M. (1993). Couples group psychotherapy. In H. I. Kaplan and B. J. Sadock (Eds.), *Comprehensive Group Psychotherapy* (3rd ed., pp. 283–292). Baltimore: Williams and Wilkins.

Cohen, S., Kamarck, T., & Mermelstein, R. A global measure of perceived stress. (1983). *Journal of Health and Social Behavior, 24*, 385–396.

Cohen, S. R., Mount, B. M., Strobel, M. G., & Bui, F. (1995). The McGill Quality of Life Questionnaire: a measure of quality of life appropriate for people with advanced disease. A preliminary study of validity and acceptability. *Palliative Medicine, 9(3)*, 207–19.

Dalton, J. A., Keefe, F. J., Carlson, J., & Youngblood, R. (2004) Tailoring cognitive-behavioral treatment for cancer pain. *Pain Management Nursing, 5(1)*, 3–18.

Dies, R. R. (1993). Research on group psychotherapy: Overview and clinical applications. In A. Alonso & H. Swiller (Eds.), *Group therapy in clinical practice*. Washington, DC: American Psychiatric Press.

Doorenbos, A., Given, B., Given, C., Verbitsky, N., Cimprich, B., & McCorkle, R. (2005). Reducing symptom limitations: a cognitive behavioral intervention randomized trial. *Psychooncology, 14(7)*, 574–584.

Eisler, R. M., Skidmore, J. R., & Ward, C. H. (1988). Masculine gender-role stress: Predictor of anger, anxiety, and health-risk behaviors. *Journal of Personality Assessment, 52*, 133–141.

Endicott, J., Nee, J., Harrison, W., & Blumenthal, R. (1993). The Quality of Life Enjoyment and Satisfaction Questionnaire. *Psychopharmacology Bulletin, 29(2)*, 321–6.

Flanigan, B. (1994). *Forgiving the unforgivable: Overcoming the bitter legacy of intimate wounds.* New York: Wiley.

Folkman, S., & Lazarus, R. (1988). *Ways of Coping Questionnaire.* Palo Alto, CA: Mind Garden.

Folstein, M.F., Robins, L.N., & Helzer, J.E. (1983). The Mini-Mental Status Examination. Social Support, Depression, and Mortality During the First Year After Myocardial Infarction. *Archives of General Psychiatry, 40(7),* 812.

Frasure-Smith, N., Lespérance, F., Gravel, G., Masson, A., Juneau, M., Talajic, M., & Bourassa, M.G. (2000). Social Support, Depression, and Mortality During the First Year After Myocardial Infarction. Circulation, *101,* 1919–1924.

Fredrickson, B. L. (2001). The role of positive emotions in positive psychology: The broaden-and-build theory of positive emotions. American Psychologist, 56, 218–226.

Gift, A. G., Moore, T., & Soeken, K. (1992). Relaxation to reduce dyspnea and anxiety in COPD patients. *Nursing Research, 41(4),* 242–246.

Greenberger, D., & Padesky, C. (1995). *Mind over mood: Change how you feel by changing the way you think.* New York: Guilford Press.

Hayes, P., & Iwamasa, G. (2006). *Culturally responsive cognitive-behavioral therapy: Assessment, practice, and supervision.* Washington, DC: American Psychological Association.

Higgins, G. O. (1994). *Resilient adults: Overcoming a cruel past.* San Francisco: Jossey-Bass.

Iribarren, C., Jacobs, D.R., Kiefe, C.I., Lewis, C.E., Matthews, K.A., Roseman, J.M., & Hulley, S.B. (2005). Causes and demographic, medical, lifestyle and psychosocial predictors of premature mortality: the CARDIA study. *Social Science & Medicine, 60(3),* 471–82.

Iribarren, C., Sidney, S., Bild, D. E., Liu, K., Markovitz, J. H., Roseman, J. M., & Matthews, K. (2000). Association of hostility with coronary artery calcification in young adults: The CARDIA study. Coronary Artery Risk Development in Young Adults. *Journal of the American Medical Association, 283(19),* 2546–2551.

Kagawa-Singer, M., & Blackhall, L. J. (2001). Negotiating cross-cultural issues at the end of life: "You got to go where he lives." *Journal of the American Medical Association, 286(23),* 2993–3001.

Kaltenthaler, E., Brazier, J., De Nigris, E., Tumur, I., Ferriter, M., Beverley, C., Parry, G., Rooney, G., & Sutcliffe, P. (2006). Computerised cognitive behaviour therapy for depression and anxiety update: A systematic review and economic evaluation. Health Technology Assessment, 10(33), iii, xi–xiv, 1–168.

Kaplan, H. I., & Sadock, B. J. (Eds.) (1993). *Comprehensive Group Psychotherapy* (3rd ed.). Baltimore: Williams and Wilkins.

Kiecolt-Glaser, J. K., Marucha, P. T., Malarkey, W. B., Mercado, A. M., & Glaser, R. (1995). Slowing of wound healing by psychological stress. *Lancet, 346,* 1194–1196.

Kiecolt-Glaser, J. K., McGuire, L., Robles, T. F., & Glaser, R. (2002). Psychoneuroimmunology: Psychological influences on immune function and health. *Journal of Consulting and Clinical Psychology, 70,* 537–547.

Kinlaw, K. (2005). Ethical issues in palliative care. *Seminars in Oncology Nursing, 221(1),* 63–68.

Kivlighan, D. M., Corazinni, J. G., & McGovern, T. V. (1985). Pregroup training. *Small Group Behavior, 16,* 500–514.

Kübler-Ross, E. (1997). *On Death and Dying.* New York: Scribner.

Kunik, M. E., Braun, U., Stanley, M. A., Wristers, K., Molinari, V., Stoebner, D., & Orengo, C. A. (2001). One session cognitive behavioural therapy for elderly patients with chronic obstructive pulmonary disease. *Psychological Medicine, 31(4),* 717–723.

Lazarus, R. S., & Folkman, S. (1984). *Stress, appraisal, and coping.* New York: Springer.

Luskin, F., Reitz, M., Newell, K., Quinn, T. G., & Haskell, W. A. (2002). Controlled pilot study of stress management training of elderly patients with congestive heart failure. *Preventive Cardiology, 5(4),* 168–172.

Lynn, J., & Harrold, J. (1999). *Handbook for mortals: Guidance for people facing serious illness.* New York: Oxford University Press.

Maslow, A. (1943). A theory of human motivation. *Psychological Review, 50,* 370–396.

McFarlane, R., & Bashe, P. (1998). *The complete bedside companion: No-nonsense advice on caring for the seriously ill.* New York: Simon & Schuster.

McGinnis, M., & Foege, W. (1993). Actual causes of death. *Journal of the American Medical Association, 270,* 2207–2212.

McKay, M., Davis, M., & Fanning, P. (2007). *Thoughts and feelings: Taking control of your moods and your life* (3rd ed.). Oakland, CA: New Harbinger Publications.

Minuchin, S. (1977). *Families and family therapy.* New York: Routledge.

Mohr, D. C., Hart, S. L., Julian, L., Catledge, C., Honos-Webb, L., Vella, L., & Tasch, E. T. (2005). Telephone-administered psychotherapy for depression. *Archives of General Psychiatry, 62(9),* 1007–1014.

Mookadam, F., & Arthur, H.M. (2004). Social Support and Its Relationship to Morbidity and Mortality After Acute Myocardial Infarction. Systematic Overview. *Archives of Internal Medicine,164,* 1514–1518.

Muñoz, R. F., & Miranda, J. (1994). SFGH Depression Clinic Group Treatment Manual. Unpublished manuscript.

Muñoz, R. F., Ying, Y. W., Bernal, G., Perez-Stable, E. J., Sorensen, J. L., Hargreaves, W. A., Miranda, J., & Miller, L. S. (1995). Prevention of depression with primary care patients: A randomized controlled trial. *American Journal of Community Psychology, 23(2),* 199–222.

Nezu, A. M. (1986). Efficacy of a social problem-solving therapy approach for unipolar depression. *Journal of Consulting and Clinical Psychology, 54(2),* 196–202.

Perkins, D. F., & Jones, K. R. (2004). Risk behaviors and resiliency within physically abused adolescents. Child Abuse & Neglect , 28(5 ), 547–563.

Petrie, K. J., Fontanilla, I., Thomas, M. G., Booth, R. J., & Pennebaker, J. W. (2004). Effect of written emotional expression on immune function in patients with human immunodeficiency virus infection: A randomized trial. *Psychosomatic Medicine, 66(2),* 272–275.

Piper, W. E., & Perrault, E. L. (1989). Pretherapy preparation for group members. *International Journal of Group Psychotherapy, 39,* 17–34.

Rabow, M., Dibble, S., Pantilat, S., & McPhee, S. (2004). The comprehensive care team: A controlled trial of outpatient palliative medicine consultation. *Archives of Internal Medicine,* 164, 83–91.

Rabow, M. W., Hauser, J. M., & Adams, J. (2004). Supporting family caregivers at the end of life: "They don't know what they don't know." *Journal of the American Medical Association, 291(4),* 483–491.

Robergs, R. A., & Roberts, S. (1997). *Exercise Physiology: Sports, Performance and Clinical Applications.* St. Louis, MO: Mosby Year-Book.

Rutan, J. S., & Stone, W. N. (2000). *Psychodynamic group psychotherapy* (3rd ed.). New York: Guilford.

Salvendy, J. T. (1993). Selection and preparation of patients and organization of the group. In H. I. Kaplan and B. J. Sadock (Eds.), *Comprehensive Group Psychotherapy* (pp. 72–83). Baltimore: Williams and Wilkins.

Sandgren, A. K., & McCaul, K. D. (2007) Long-term telephone therapy outcomes for breast cancer patients. *Psychooncology, 16(1),* 38–47.

Satterfield, J. M. (1994). Integrating group dynamics and cognitive-behavioral groups: A hybrid model. *Clinical Psychology: Science and Practice,1,* 185–196.

Searight, H. R., & Gafford, J. (2005). Cultural diversity at the end of life: Issues and guidelines for family physicians. *American Family Physician, 71,* 515–522.

Seligman, M. E. P., Steen, T. A., Park, N., & Peterson, C. (2005). Positive psychology progress: Empirical validation of interventions. *American Psychologist, 60,* 410–421.

Seybold, K. S., & Hill, P. C. (2001). The role of religion and spirituality in mental and physical health. Current Directions in Psychological Science , *10,* 21–24.

Sherwood, P., Given, B. A., Given, C. W., Champion, V. L., Doorenbos, A. Z., Azzouz, F., Kozachik, S., Wagler-Ziner, K., & Monahan, P. O. (2005). A cognitive behavioral intervention for symptom management in patients with advanced cancer. *Oncology Nursing Forum, 32(6),* 1190–1198.

Sivertsen, B., Omvik, S., Pallesen, S., Bjorvatn, B., Havik, O. E., Kvale, G., Nielsen, G. H., & Nordhus, I. H. (2006). Cognitive behavioral therapy vs. zopiclone for treatment of chronic primary insomnia in older adults: A randomized controlled trial. *Journal of the American Medical Association, 295(24),* 2851–2858.

Snyder, C.R., & Lopez, S.J. (2005). Handbook of Positive Psychology. New York: Oxford University Press.

Spek, V., Cuijpers, P., Nyklíček, I., Riper, H., Keyzer, J., & Pop, V. (2007) Internet-based cognitive behaviour therapy for symptoms of depression and anxiety: A meta-analysis. Psychological Medicine, 37(3), 319–328.

Spiegel, D., Bloom, J. R., Kraemer, H. C., & Gottheil, E. (1989). Effect of psychosocial treatment on survival of patients with metastatic breast cancer. *The Lancet,* October 14, 1989.

Spielberger, C.D., Gorsuch, R.L., & Lushene, R.E. (1968). *State Trait Anxiety Inventory.* Palo Alto, CA: Consulting Psychololgists Press.

Spielberger, C. D., Jacobs, G., Russell, S., & Crane, R. S. (1983). Assessment of anger: The State-Trait Anger Scale. In Butcher, J. N., and Spielberger, C. D. (Eds.), *Advances in Personality Assessment* (pp. 161–189). Hillsdale, NJ: Lawrence Erlbaum Associates.

Sue, D. W., & Sue, D. (2007). *Counseling the culturally diverse.* Indianapolis, IN: Wiley.

Surtees, P. G., Wainwright, N. W., Luben, R., Day, N. E., & Khaw, K. T. (2005). Prospective cohort study of hostility and the risk of cardiovascular disease mortality. *International Journal of Cardiology,* 100(1), 155–61.

Vallis, T. M., Shaw, B. F., & Dobson, K. S. (1986). The Cognitive Therapy Scale: Psychometric properties. *Journal of Consulting and Clinical Psychology, 54(3),* 381–385.

Waltman, D. E., & Zimpfer, D. G. (1988). Composition, structure, and duration of treatment: Interacting variables in counseling groups. *Small Group Behavior, 19,* 171–184.

Werth, D., & Blevins, J. W. (Eds.) (2005). *Psychosocial issues near the end of life: A resource for professional care providers.* Washington, DC: American Psychological Association.

Yalom, I. (1985). *The theory and practice of group psychotherapy* (3rd ed.). New York: Basic Books.

Yesavage, J. A., Brink, T. L., Rose, T. L., Lum, O., Huang, V., Adey, M., & Leirer, V. O. (1982). Development and validation of a geriatric depression screening scale: a preliminary report. *Journal of Psychiatric Research, 17(1)*, 37–49.

Zilberg, N., Weiss, D., & Horowitz, M. (1982). Impact of Event Scale: a cross validation study and some empirical evidence supporting a conceptual model of stress response syndromes. Journal of Consulting and Clinical Psychology, *50*, 409–414.

Zimet, G. D., Powell, S. S., Farley, G. K., Werkman, S., & Berkoff, K. A. (1990) Psychometric characteristics of the multidimensional scale of perceived social support. *Journal of Personality Assessment, 55*, 610–617.

Zung, W. (1967). Factors influencing the Self-Rating Depression Scale. *Archives of General Psychiatry, 16*, 543–547.

# About the Authors

**Jason M. Satterfield**, Ph.D., is Associate Professor of Clinical Medicine and Director of Behavioral Medicine in the Division of General Internal Medicine at the University of California, San Francisco. He received his Ph.D. from the University of Pennsylvania in 1995, where he worked with Drs. Martin Seligman and Aaron T. Beck on cognitive models of bias, risk taking, and aggression. In 1995, Dr. Satterfield began working at San Francisco General Hospital to adapt cognitive-behavioral therapy for groups to underserved, medically ill populations. In 1998, he joined the UCSF Comprehensive Care Team, created to provide clinical consultations and psychosocial care for patients at the "beginning of the end of life." Dr. Satterfield's current interests include cognitive and explanatory models of illness, mind-body factors in health and disease, and the somatic expression of emotion. His current projects include integrated behavioral health models for primary care, cognitive-behavioral therapy for palliative care, emotional intelligence in medical providers, and the integration of culture and behavioral sciences in medical school curricula. He divides his time between ongoing patient care, teaching, and clinical research.